A Colorful World

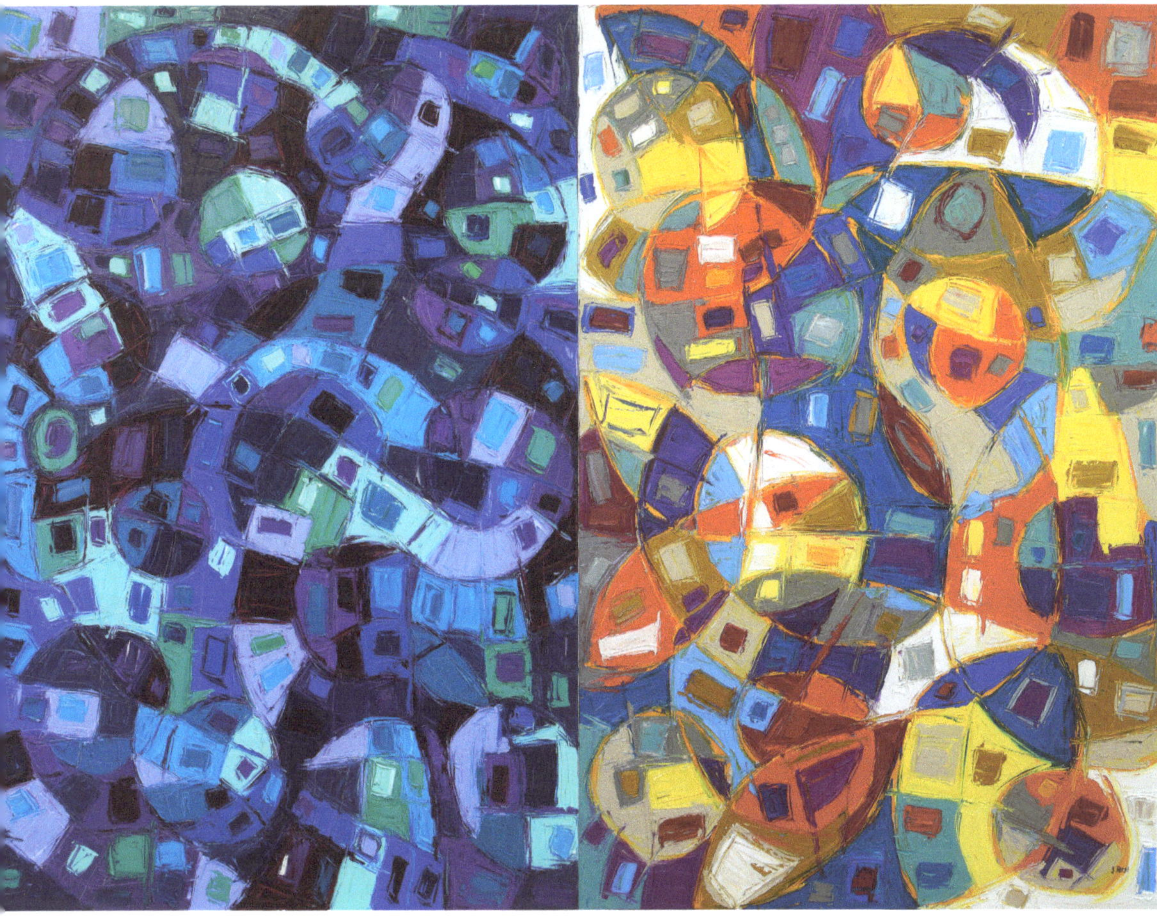

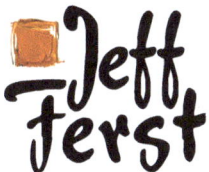

Jeff Ferst

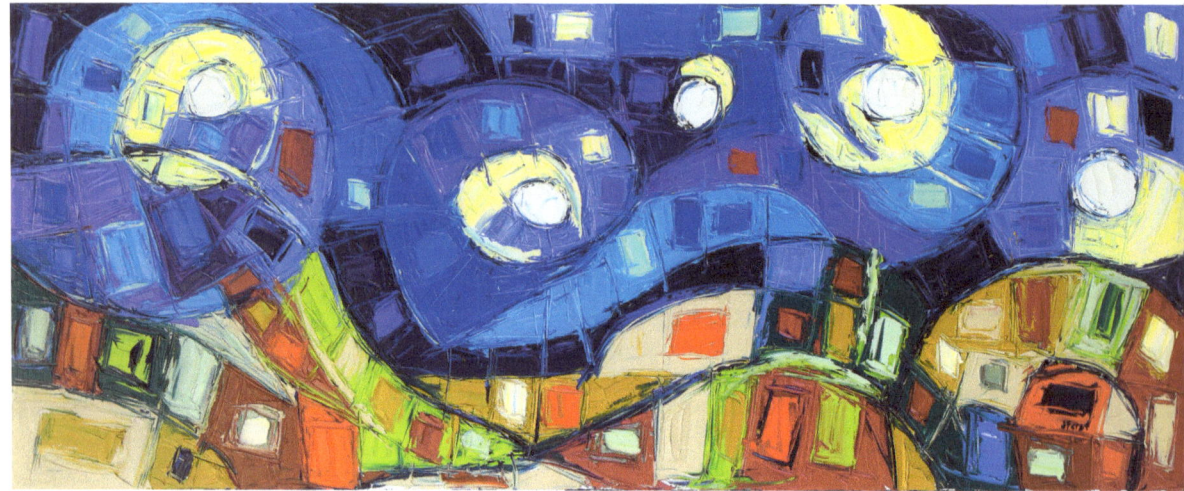

Starry Night, 24 x 60 inches, Oil on canvas, 2010

Painting is philosophy made incarnate, a sense of the world embodied in visual and material form. Painting is a guide to how we might relate to the world, as if it were a newly discovered land.

In Jeff Ferst's paintings, we encounter a world that just won't stop whirling and scintillating. More precisely, it is made of many worlds, arcing nodes that intersect with other circles to create a myriad of connections. Each world is a kind of sphere of influence, a locus of energy, but never existing independently of the entire matrix. It is that interplay that gives Ferst's paintings their distinctive, playful musicality.

Essential to the paintings' structure are the blocks of color that compose the curving circuitry. These blocks, themselves often inset with concentric squares, act like the tesserae of mosaics, simultaneously creating and deconstructing form. And they give the paintings a jewel-like quality, as if reflecting light from its complex surface.

Ferst adopts as his own a visual language derived from early modernism, particularly from Cubism, and from its ecstatic variant, Orphism. But he paints gesturally with thick pigment, and with a personal passion and energy. The structure of his "geometric landscapes" is distinctly organic, form generating form with an intuitive inner logic. The image of the garden appears as a specific subject, and as an apt metaphor for Ferst's art. He seems to be working with wild energies, and like a gardener shaping these impulses into a new state that is a melding of the natural and the aesthetic.

Within the complex fields that Ferst paints, images begin to appear. They are in a sense camouflaged, or encoded with the larger structure. An arc becomes a snake, a head appears in the overlapping of curves, faces peek from free-floating circles. Whole figures are apparent, and we become aware that Ferst's paintings teem with people or at least the evocations of individuals. We start to see the spinning worlds of his paintings as intersecting pyches, memories and spirits.

Color plays a powerful role in these works, energizing and organizing our vision. Ferst's hues are often intense, playing warm against cool, creating a pulsing visual experience. But he also allows olive, putty, rusty plum and other lower saturation colors to contrast with the higher key tones around them. The artist seems to be showing us something about an emotional undertow that coexists in the world along with the feelings of pleasure and joy.

John Mendelsohn

John Mendelsohn is a painter who has written articles and reviews on contemporary art for ArtNet, Cover Magazine, dArt International and The Jewish Week, as well as essays for exhibition catalogues. He teaches in the Studio Art Program at Fairfield University in Connecticut. He has contributed to the forthcoming book, A Book of Images: Reflections on Symbols, to be published by Taschen in conjunction with the Archive for Research in Archetypal Symbolism at the C.G. Jung Institute, New York.

Geometric Landscapes

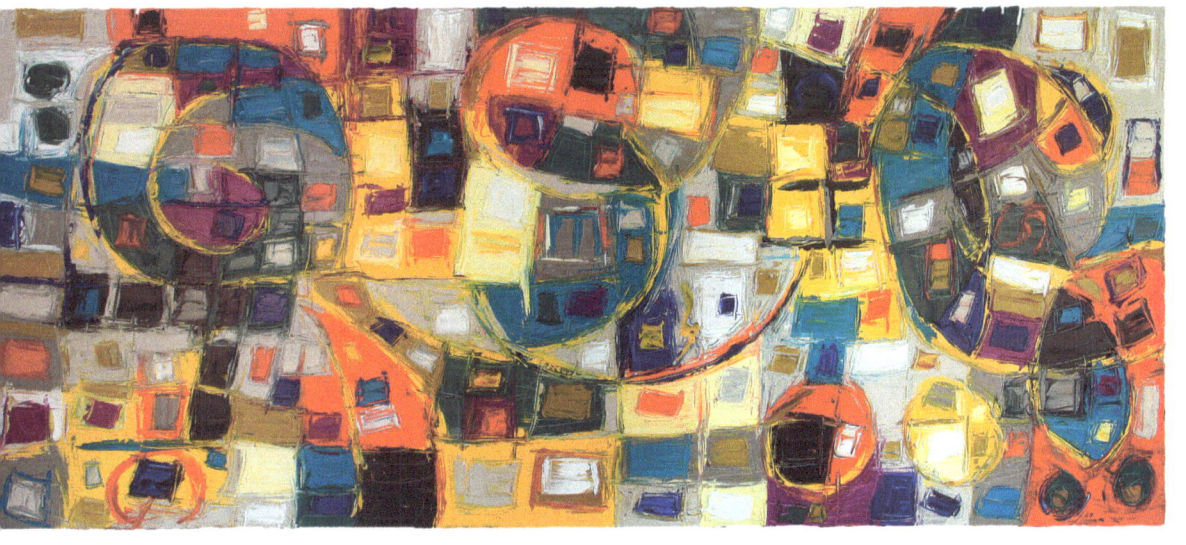

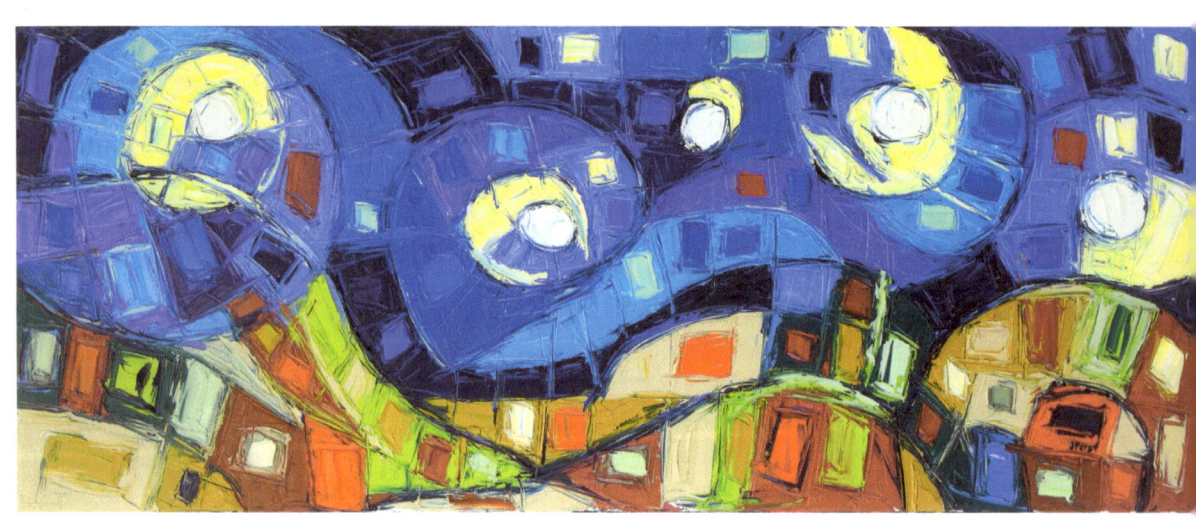

Starry Night
24 x 60 inches
Oil on canvas
2010

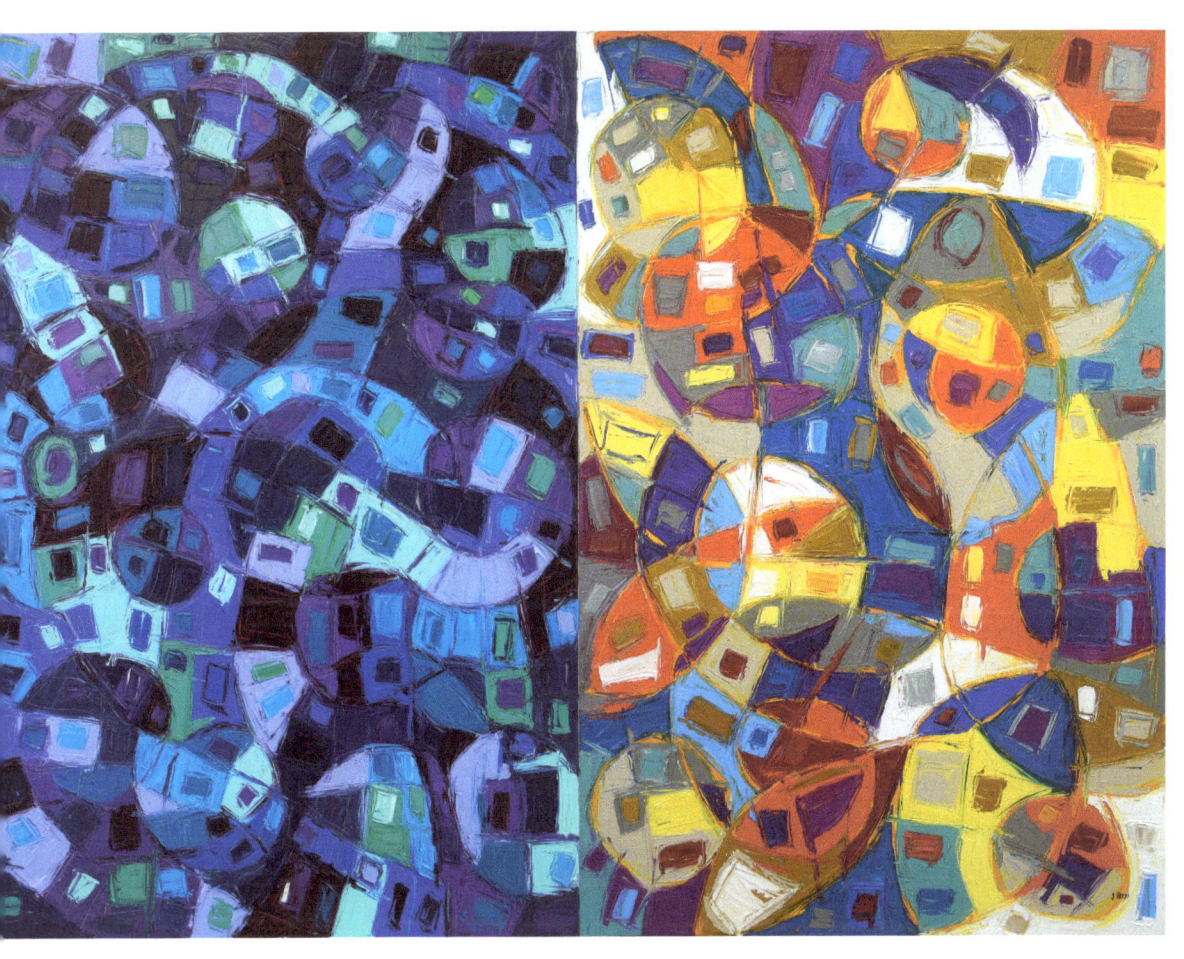

Night & Day
72 x 96 inches
Oil on canvas
2010

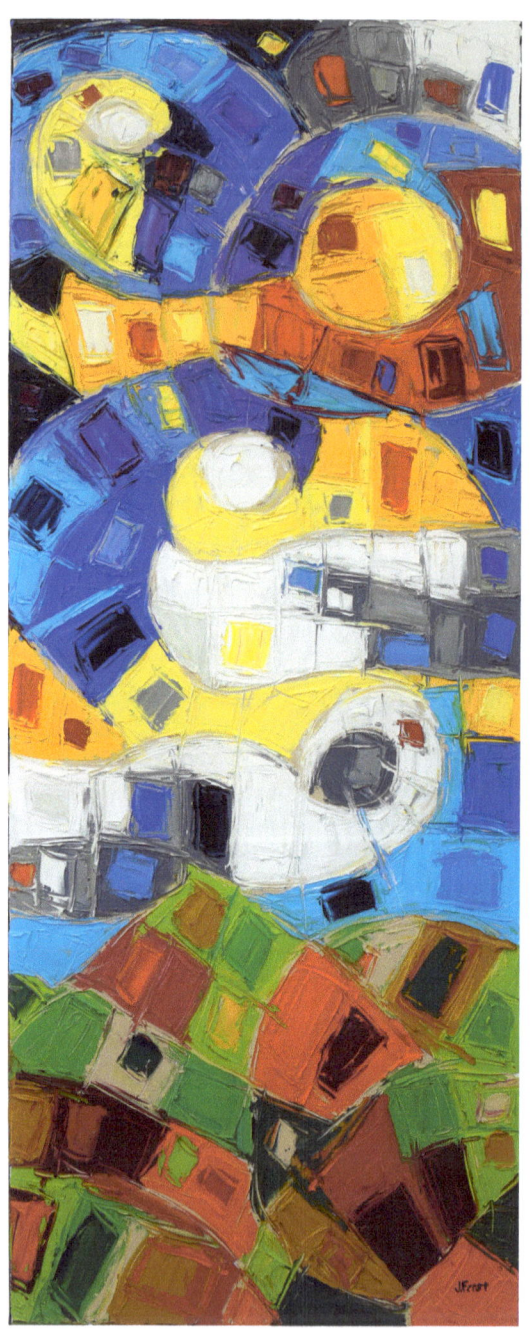

Sun & Moon
60 x 24 inches
Oil on canvas
2010

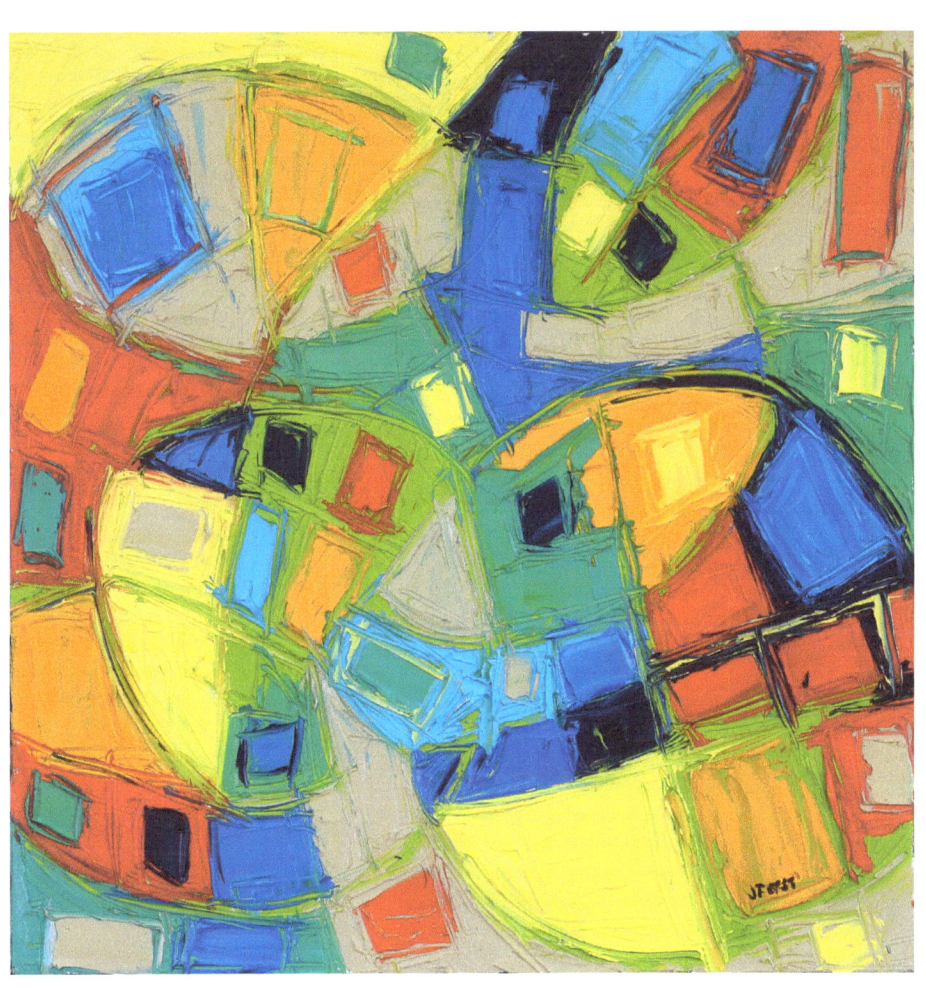

Spring Bouquet
24 x 24 inches
Oil on canvas
2010

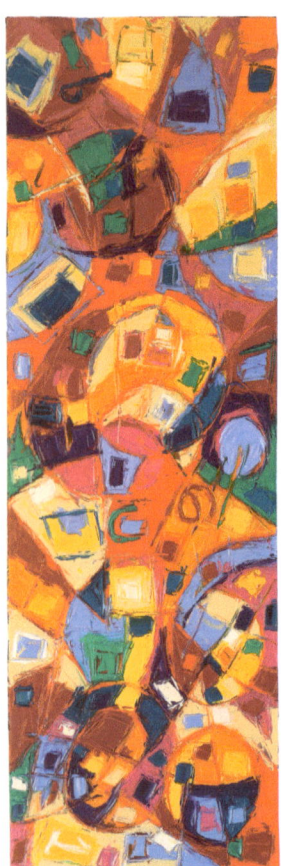 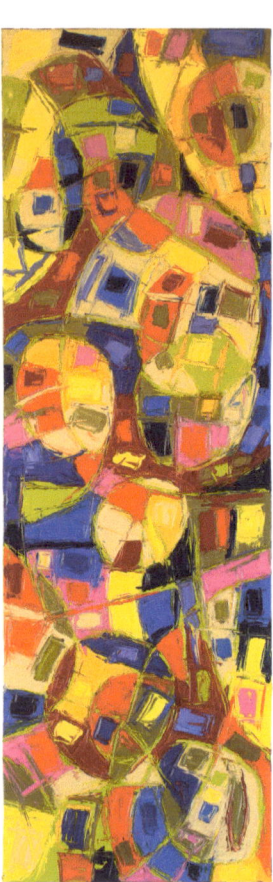 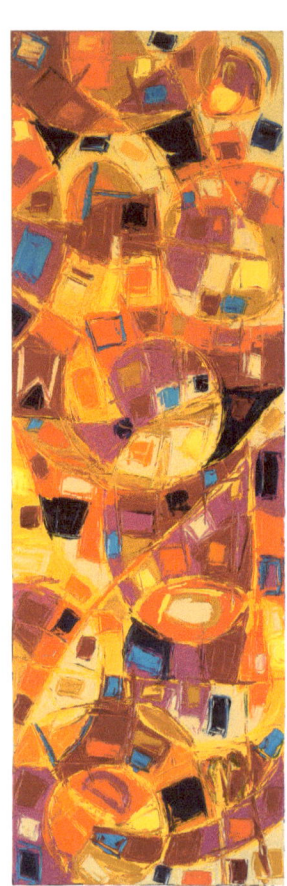 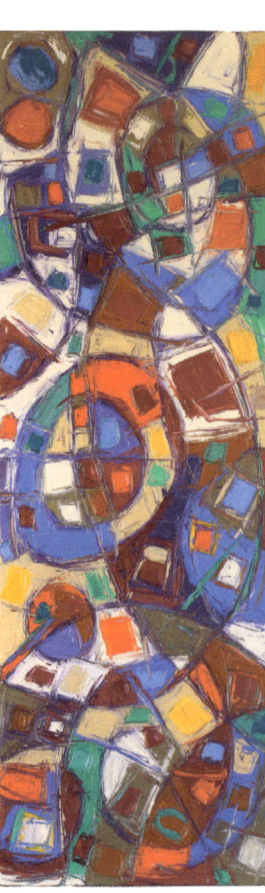

Fantasia
72 x 108 inches
Oil on canvas
2010

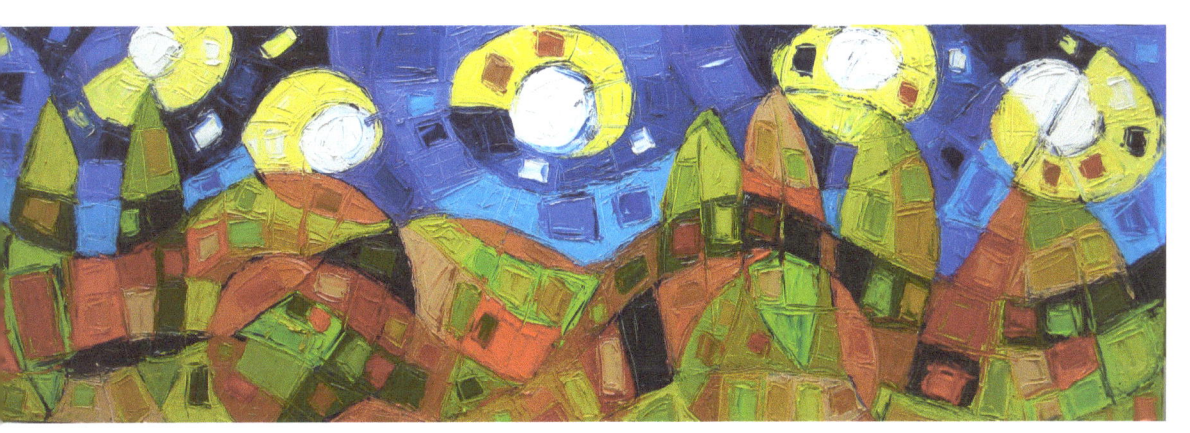

The Journey
24 x 60 inches
Oil on canvas
2010

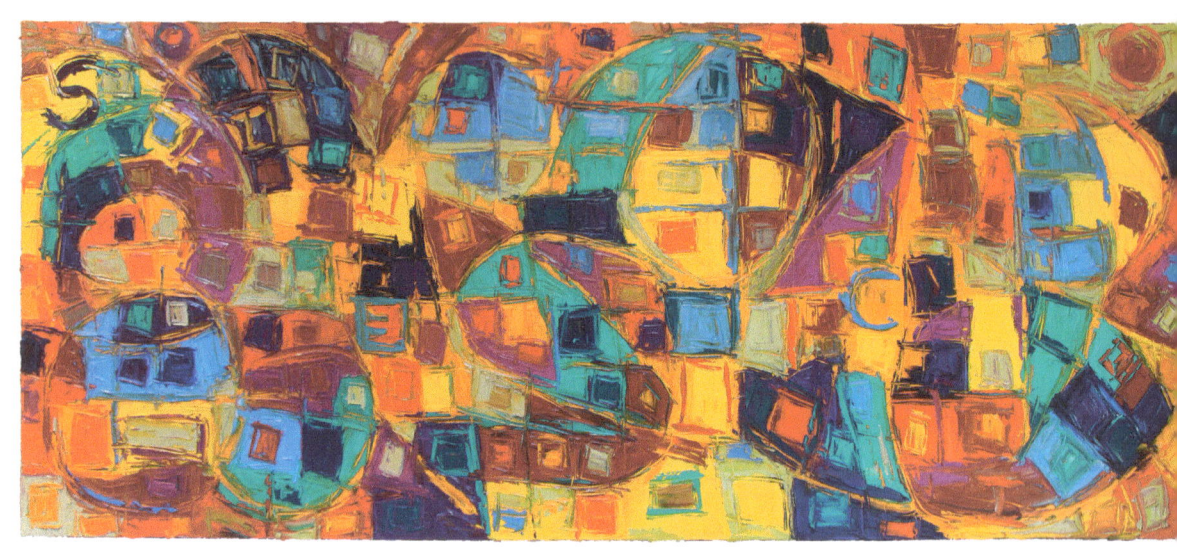

Hot Summer Nights
36 x 84 inches
Oil on canvas
2009

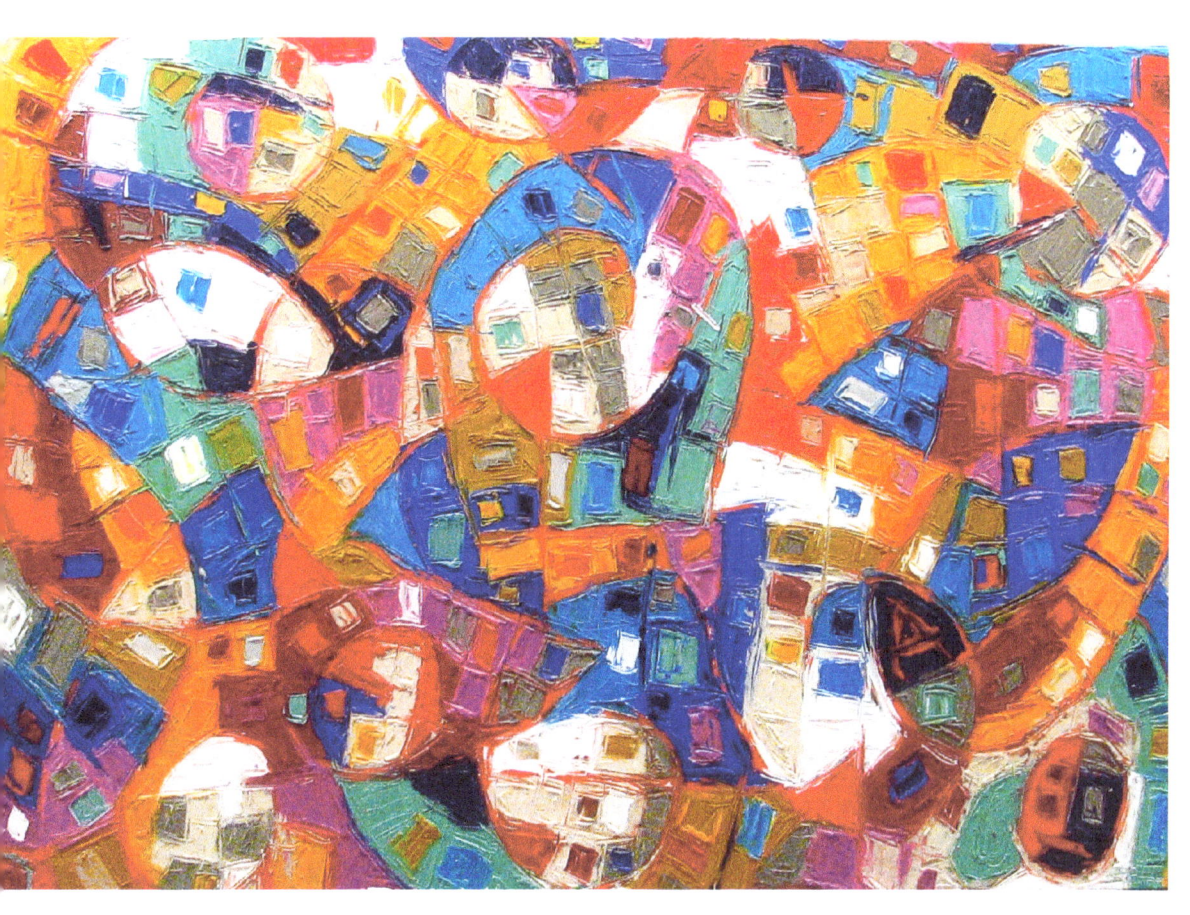

Family Ties
60 x 84 inches
Oil on canvas
2010

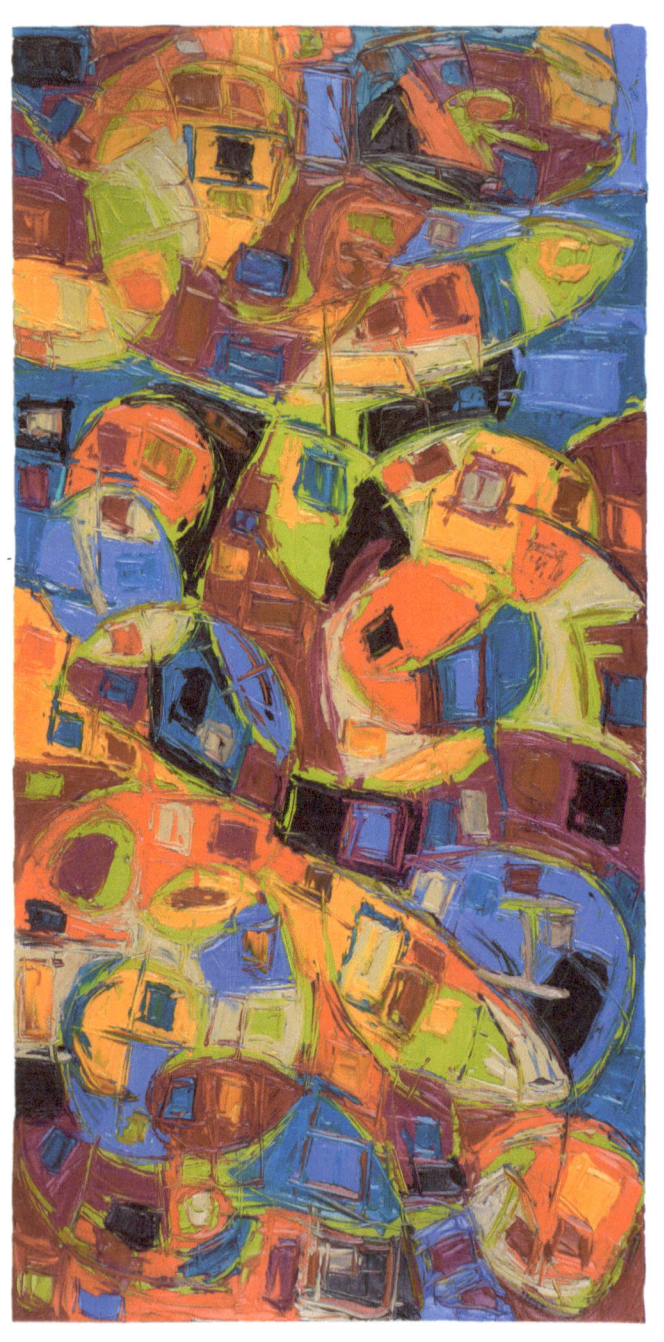

Garden Dream
60 x 30 inches
Oil on canvas
2009

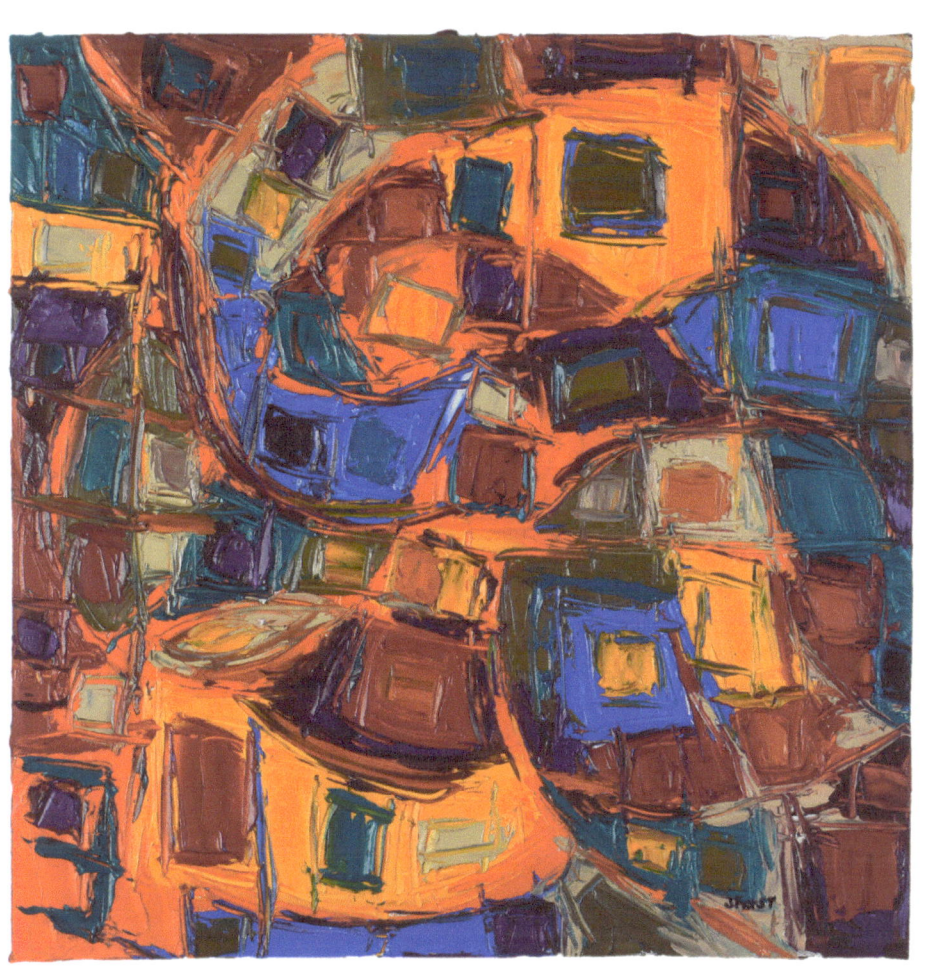

Senorran Desert
24 x 24 inches
Oil on canvas
2009

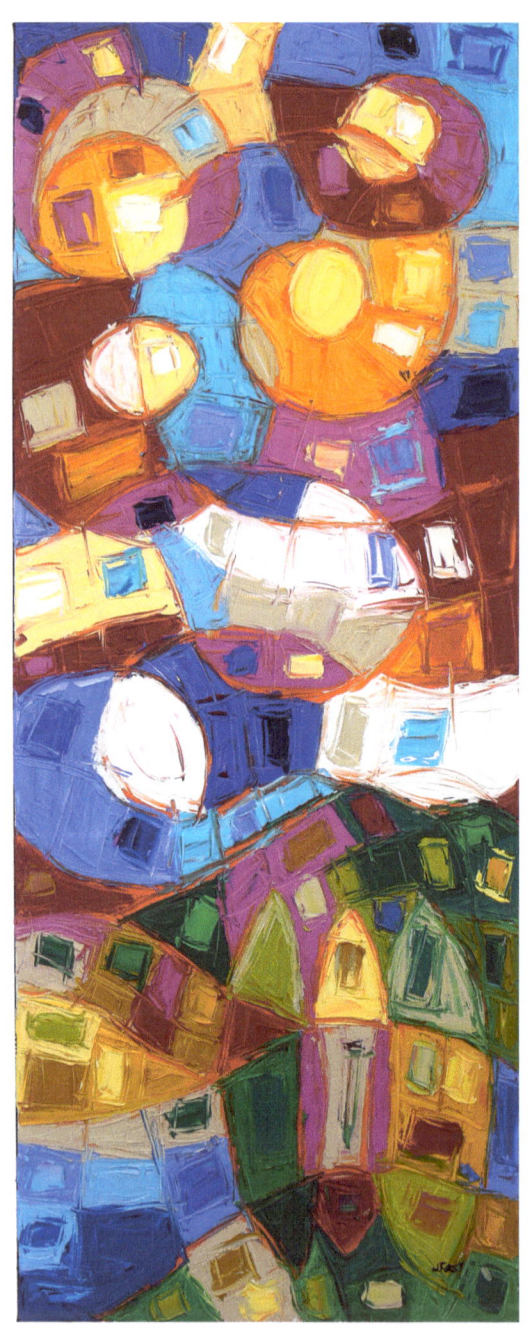

Tuscan Dawn
60 x 24 inches
Oil on canvas
2010

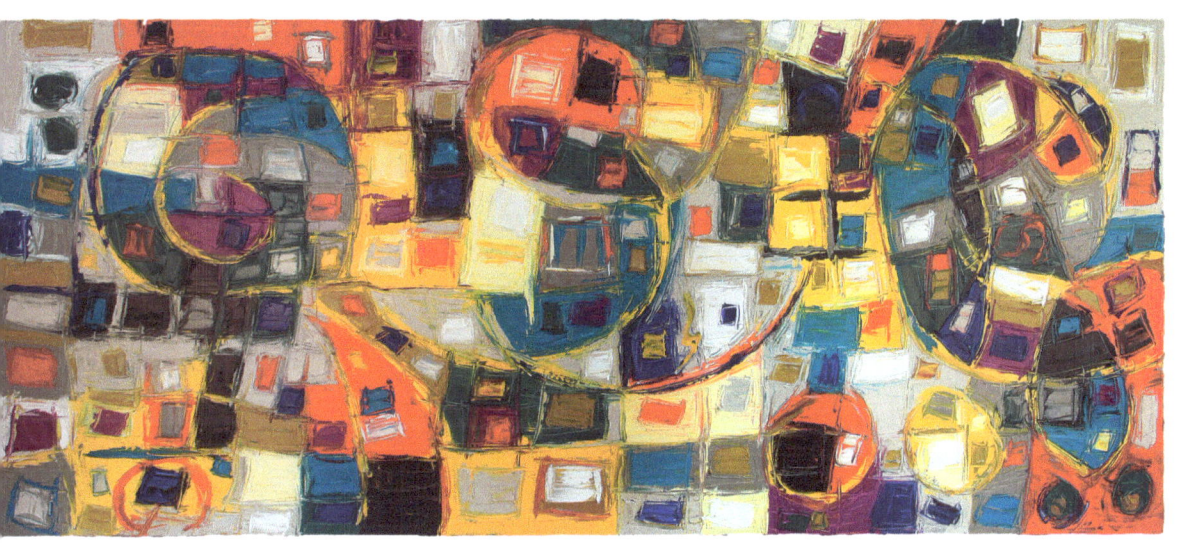

Essentially Jazz
36 x 84 inches
Oil on canvas
2009

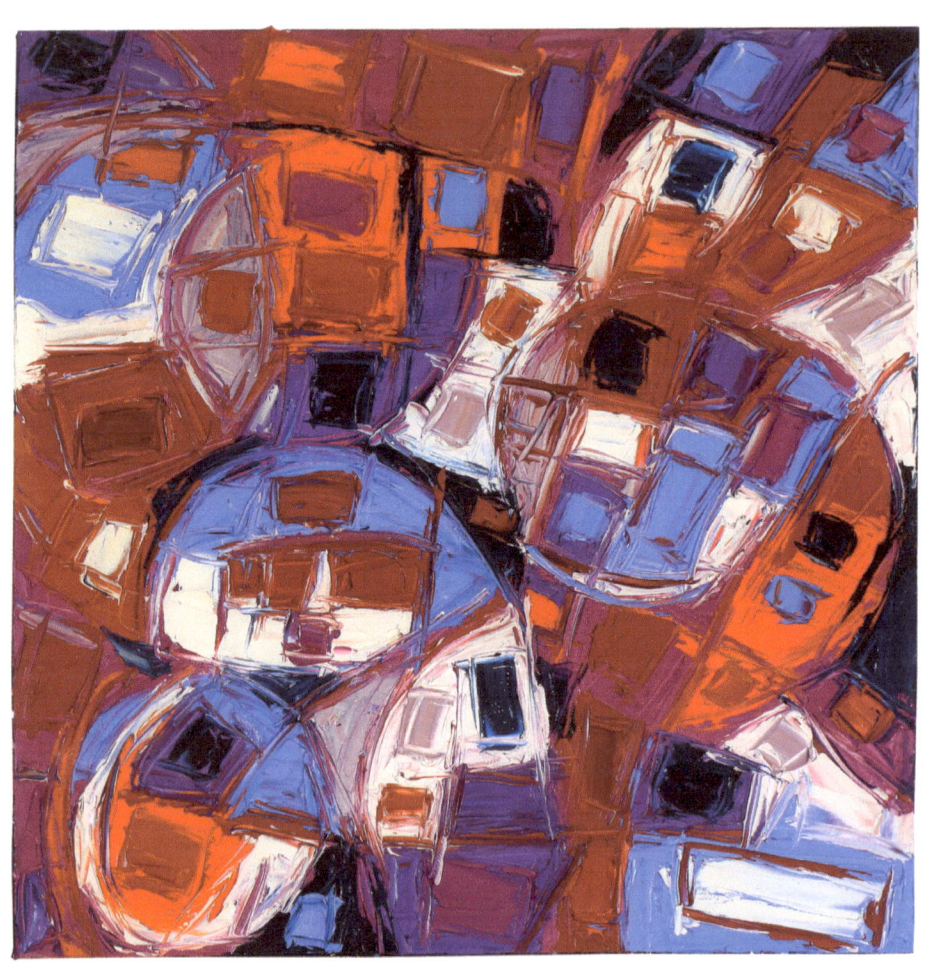

Red, White & Blue
24 x 24 inches
Oil on canvas
2010

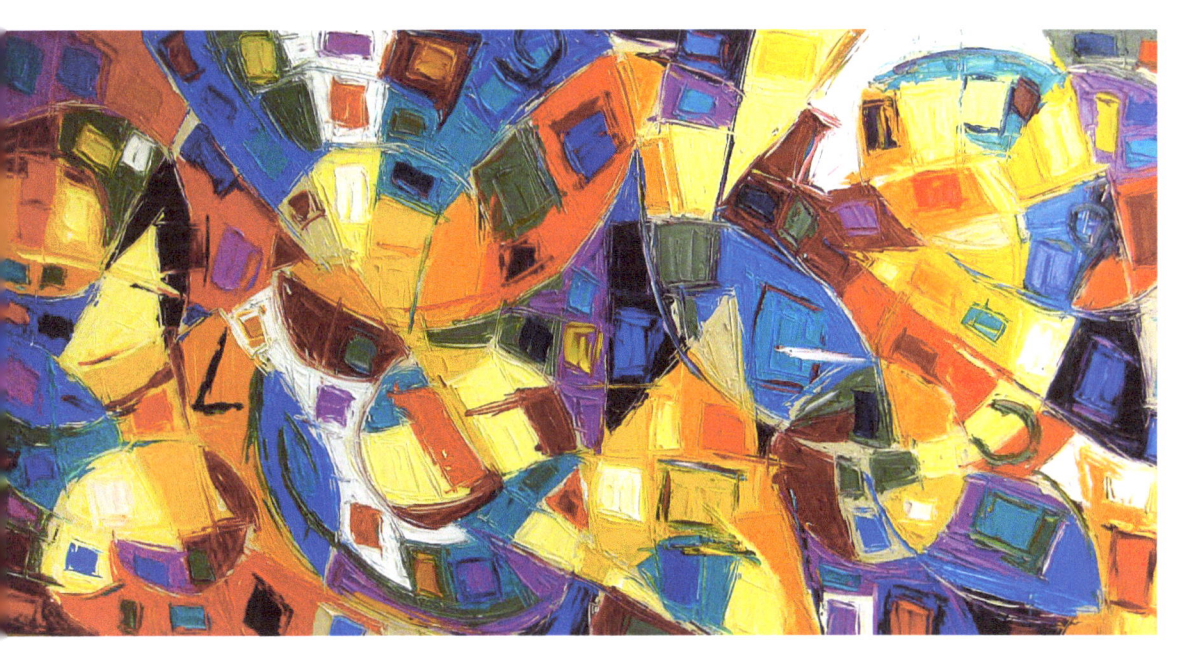

Flashback
36 x 72 inches
Oil on canvas
2010

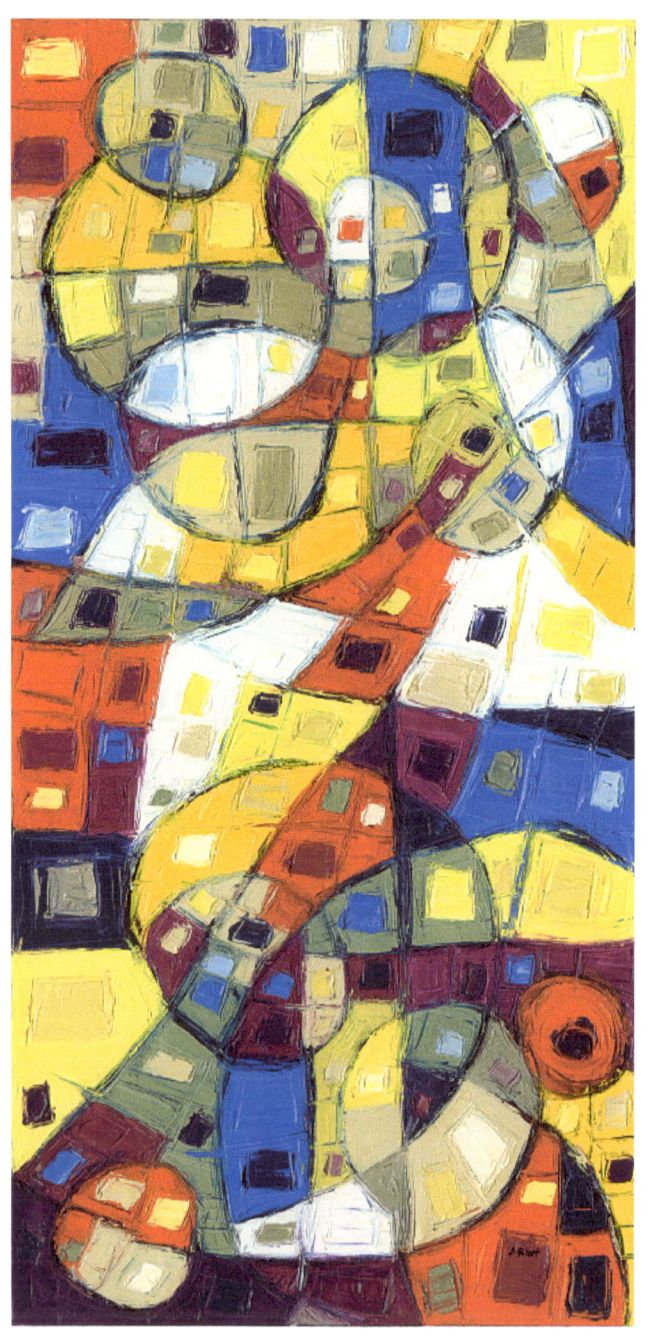

Give Me Wings to Fly
72 x 30 inches
Oil on canvas
2009

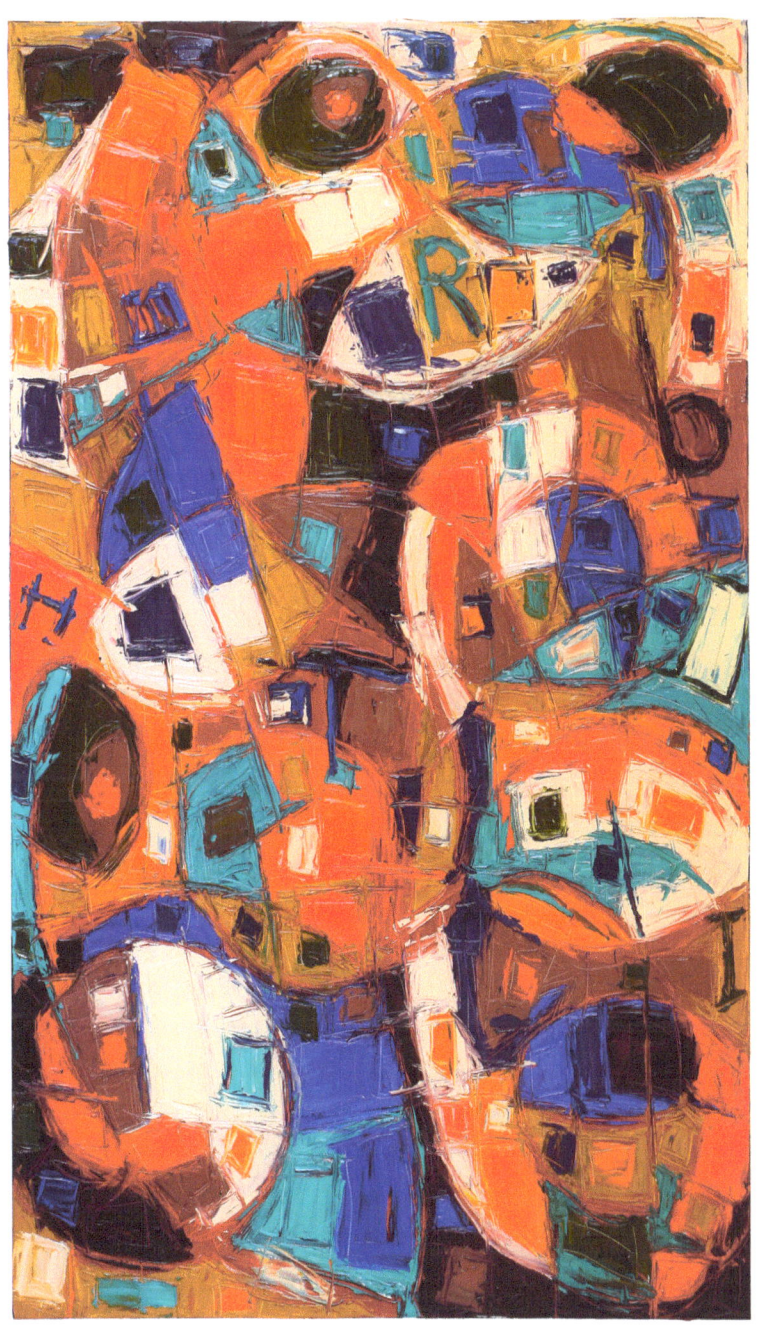

Flora & Fauna
60 x 40 inches
Oil on canvas
2009

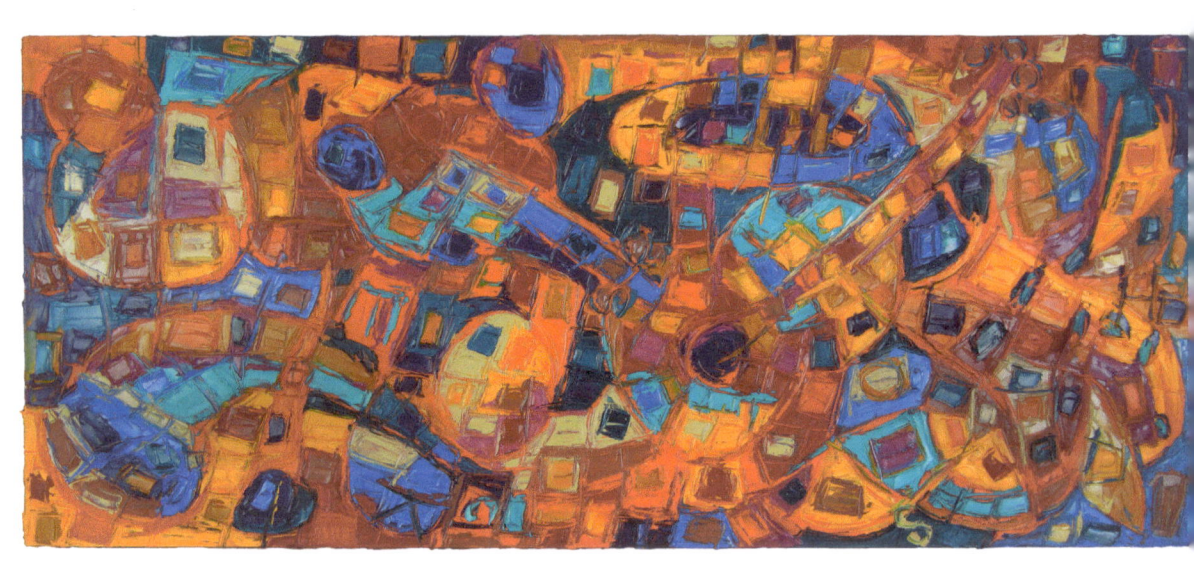

Music to My Ears
36 x 84 inches
Oil on canvas
2009

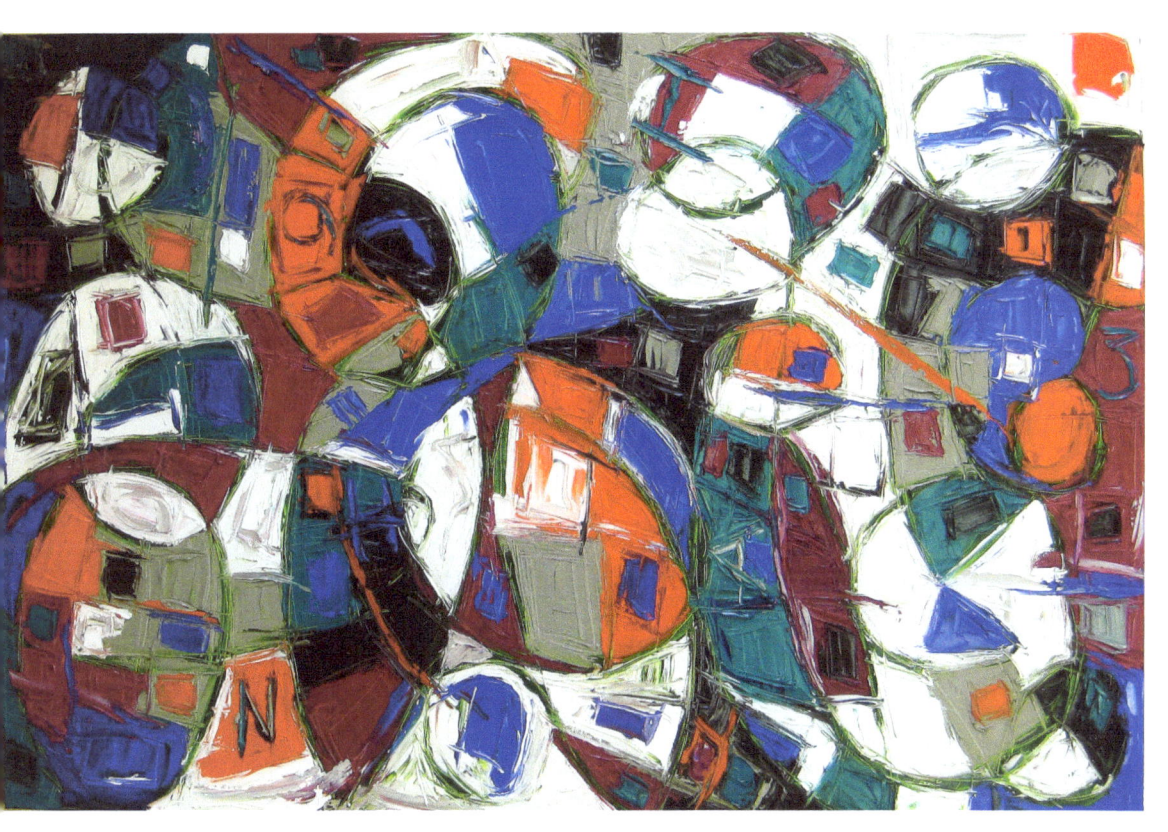

In or Out
40 x 60 inches
Oil on canvas
2009

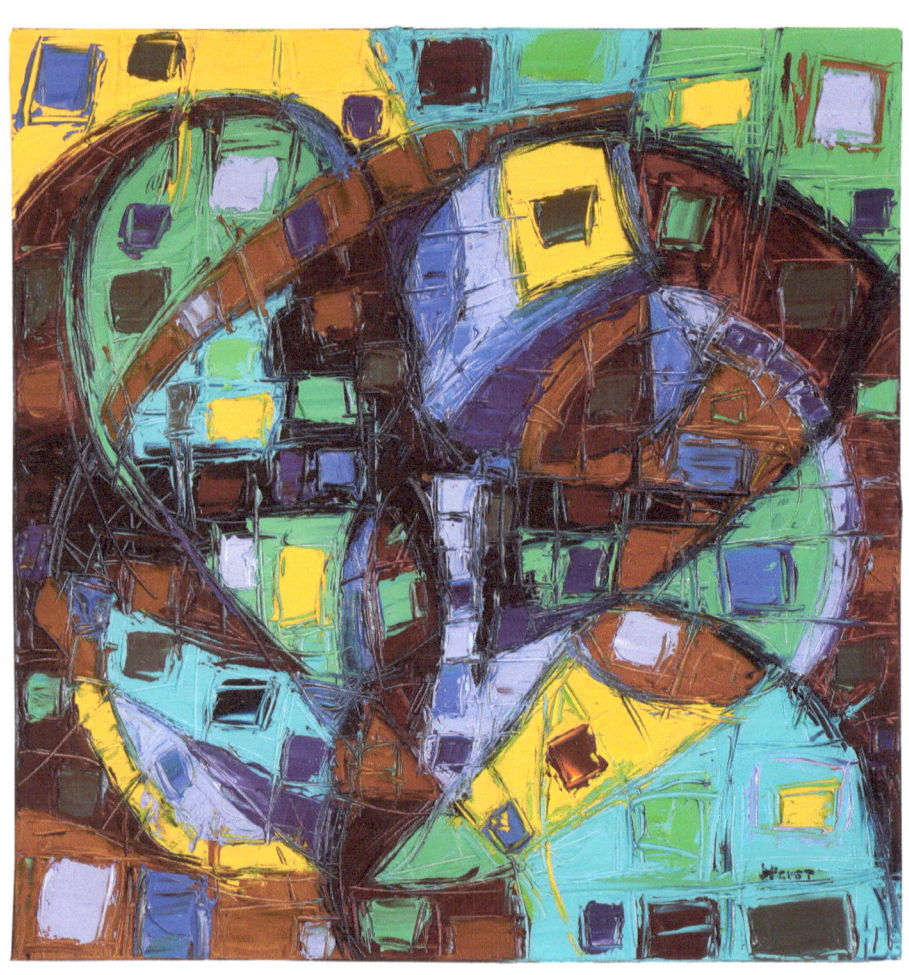

Light Side of the Moon
24 x 24 inches
Oil on canvas
2009

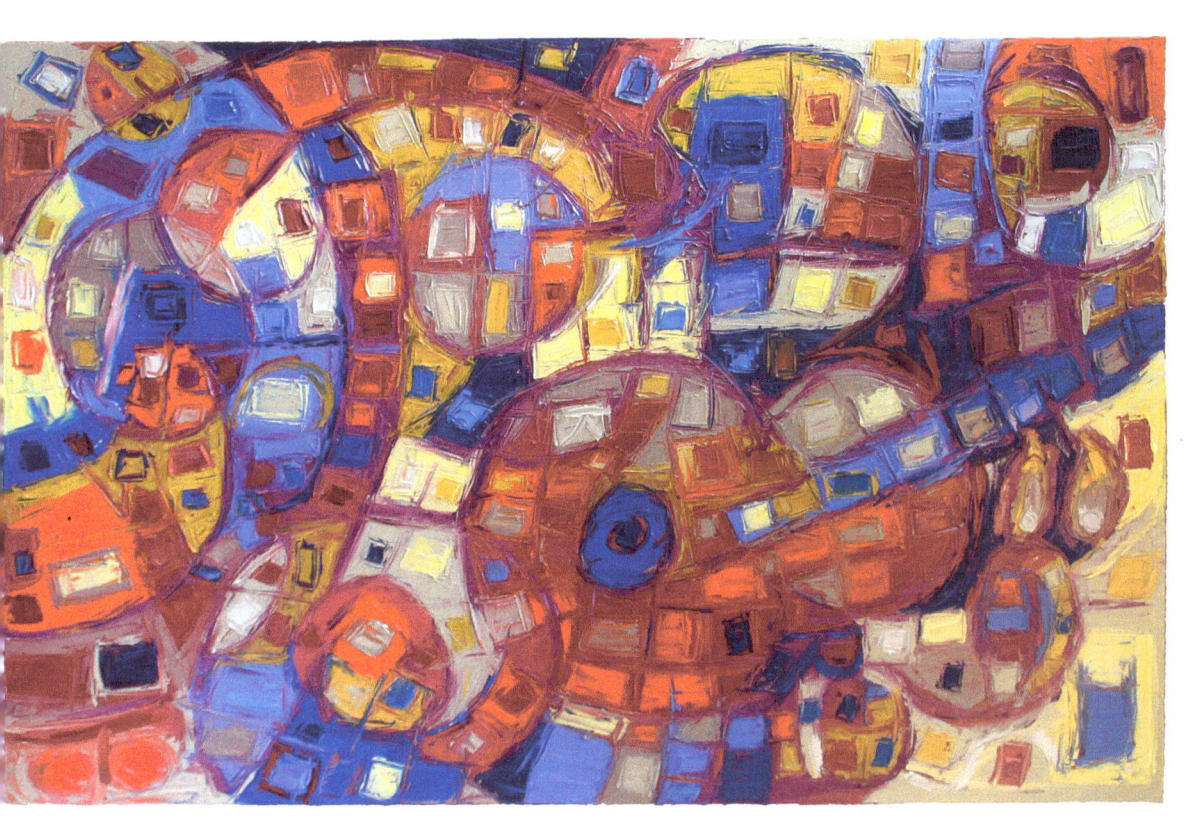

Unplugged
48 x 72 inches
Oil on canvas
2009

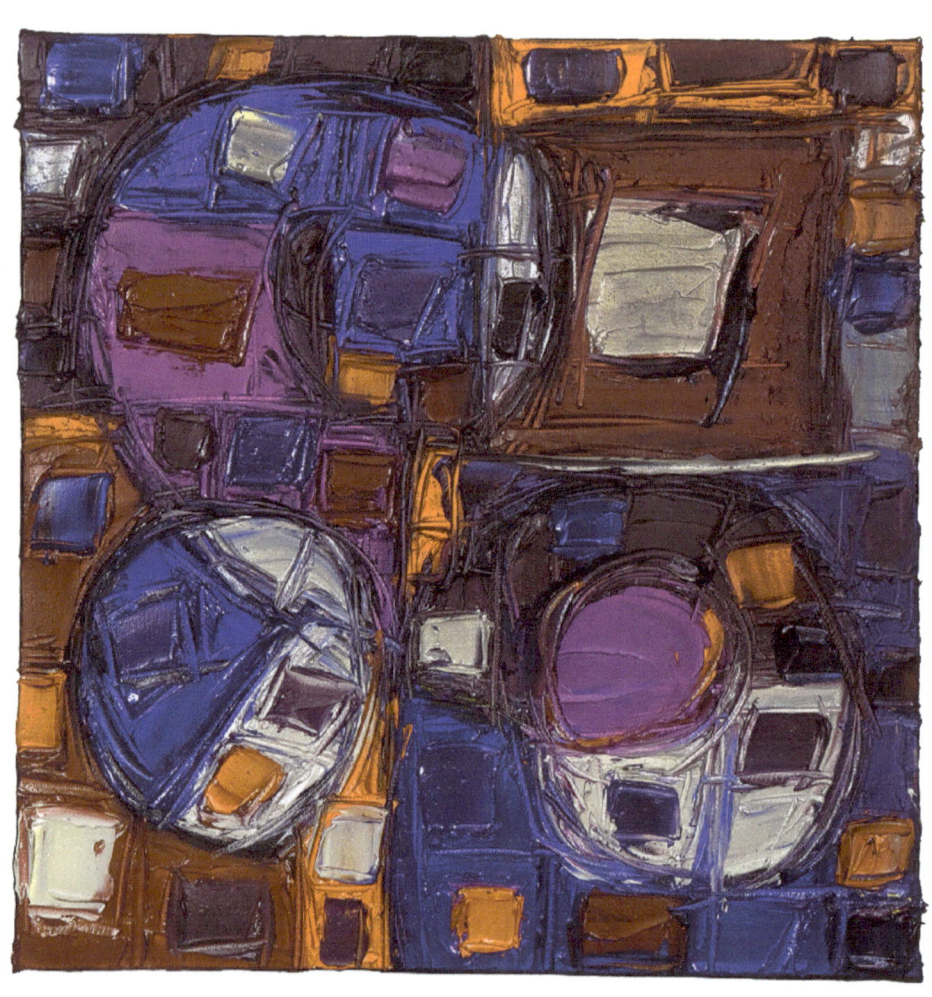

Stop The Red Lips
16 x 16 inches
Oil on canvas
2009

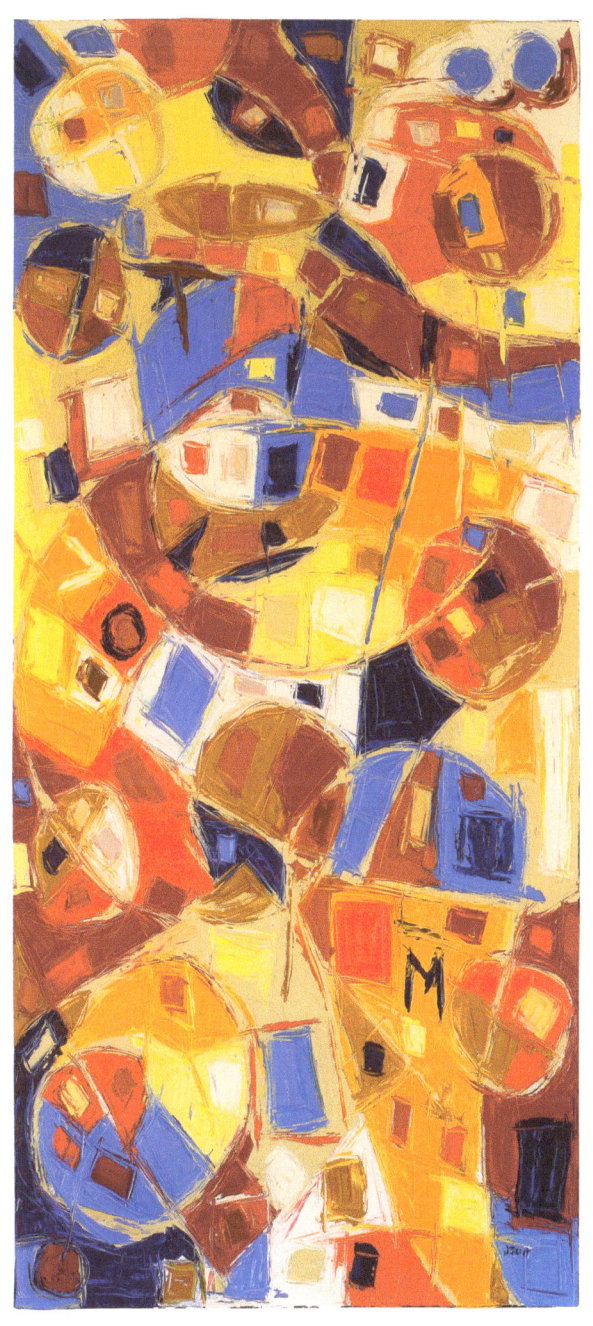

Flight of Fancy
72 x 36 inches
Oil on canvas
2010

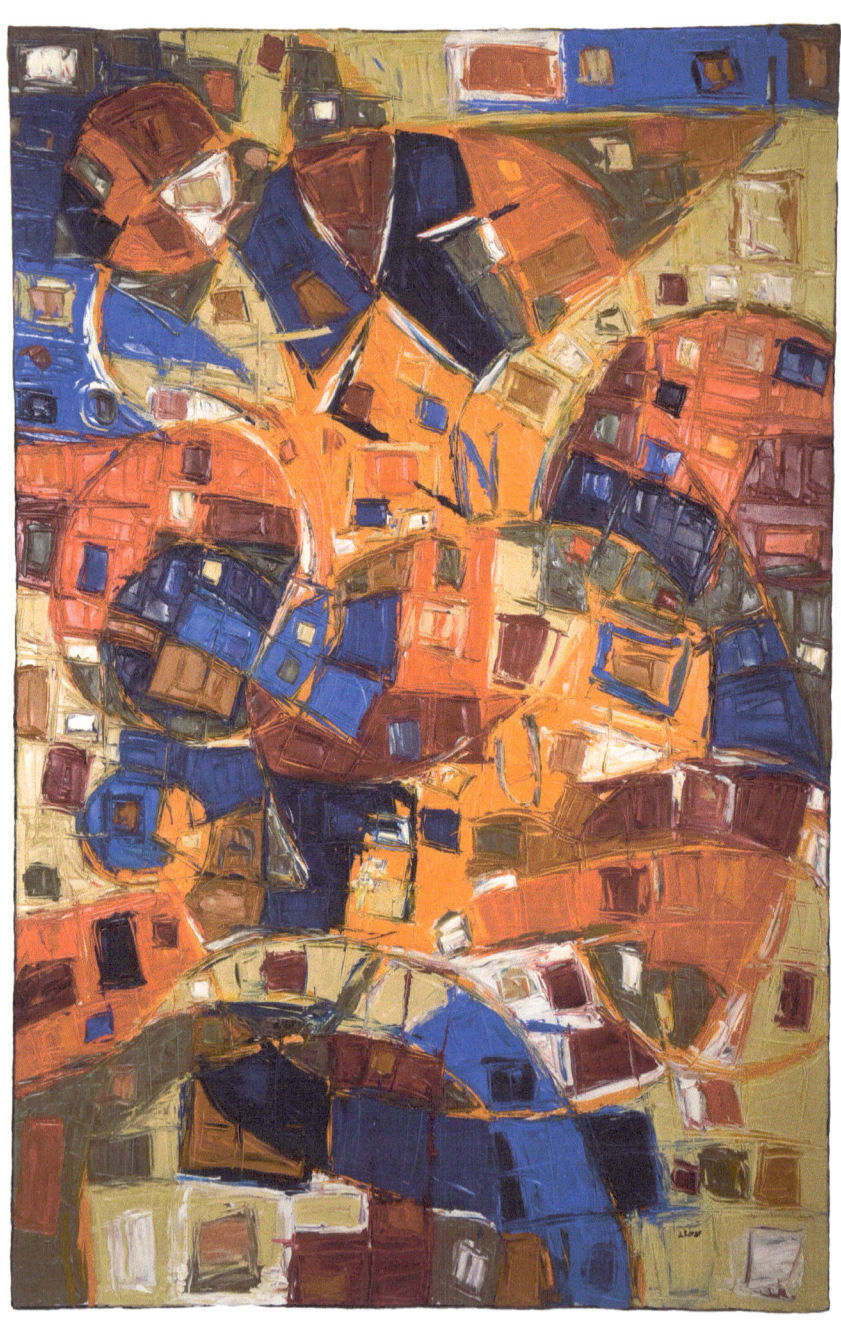

Enough
72 x 24 inches
Oil on canvas
2009

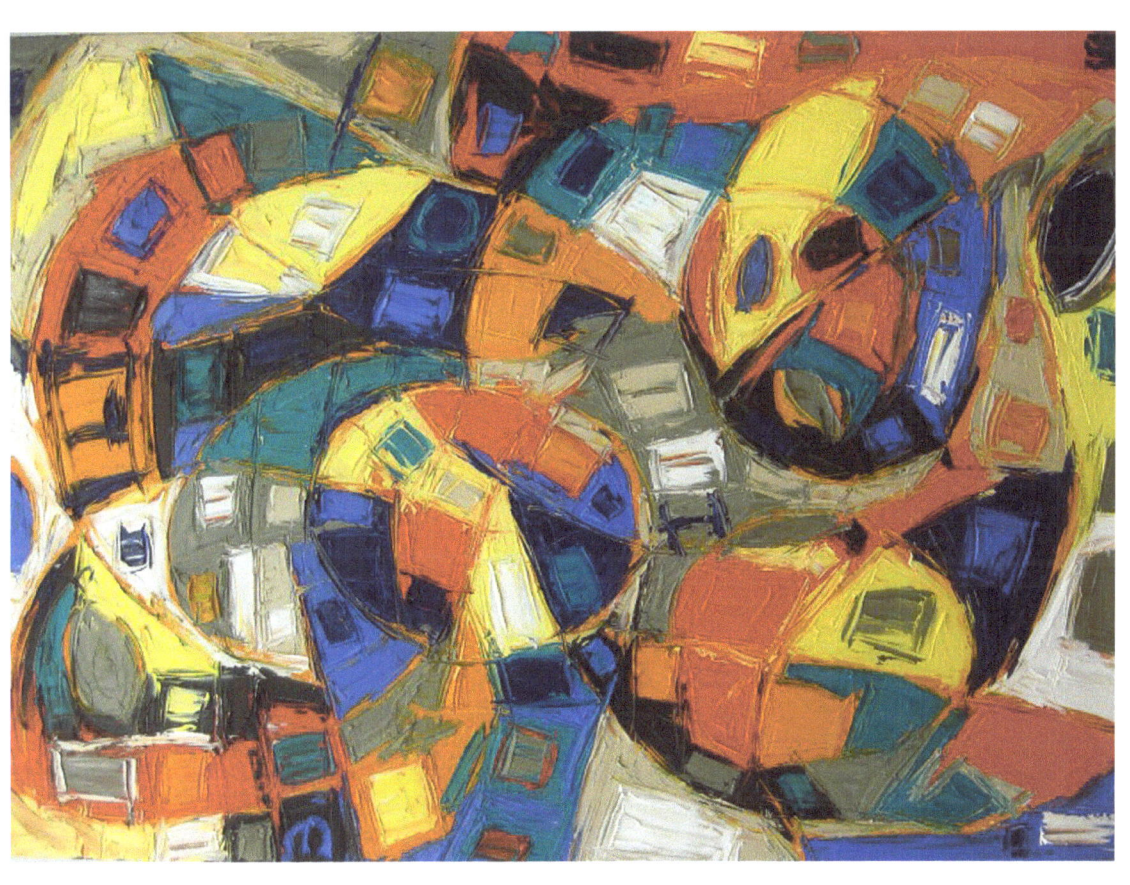

Serendipity
40 x 60 inches
Oil on canvas
2010

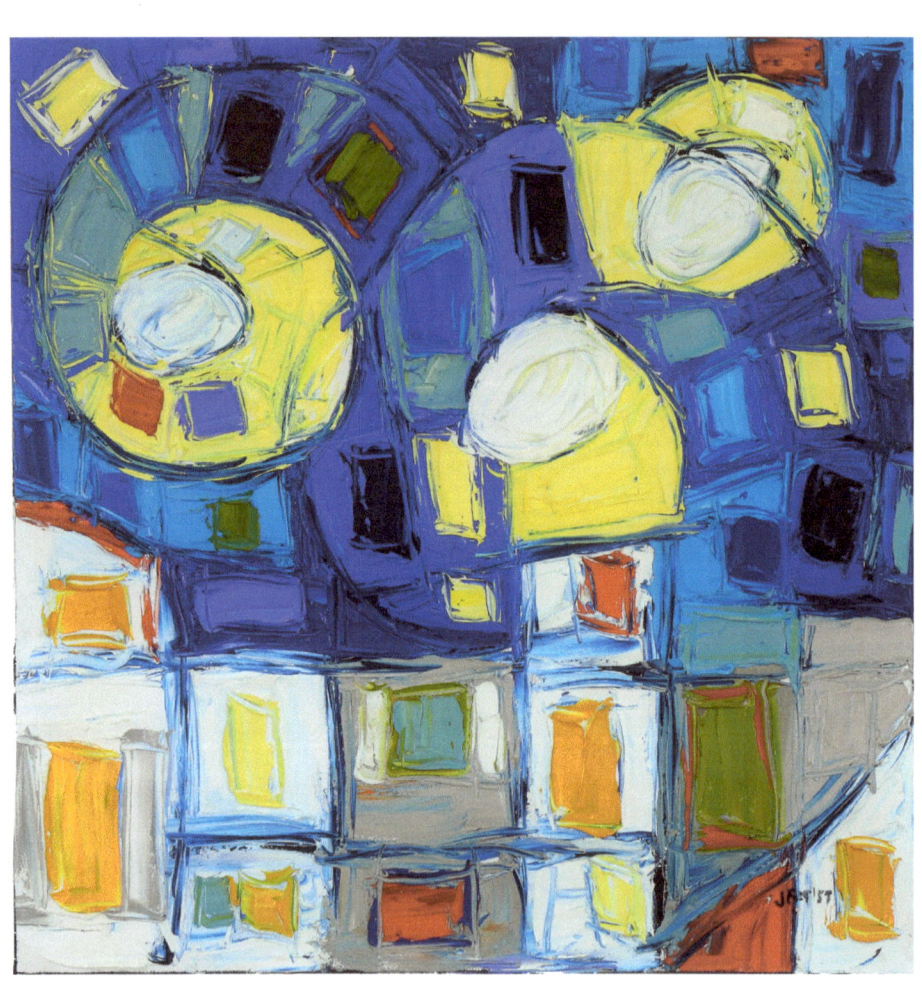

City Sky
24 x 24 inches
Oil on canvas
2010

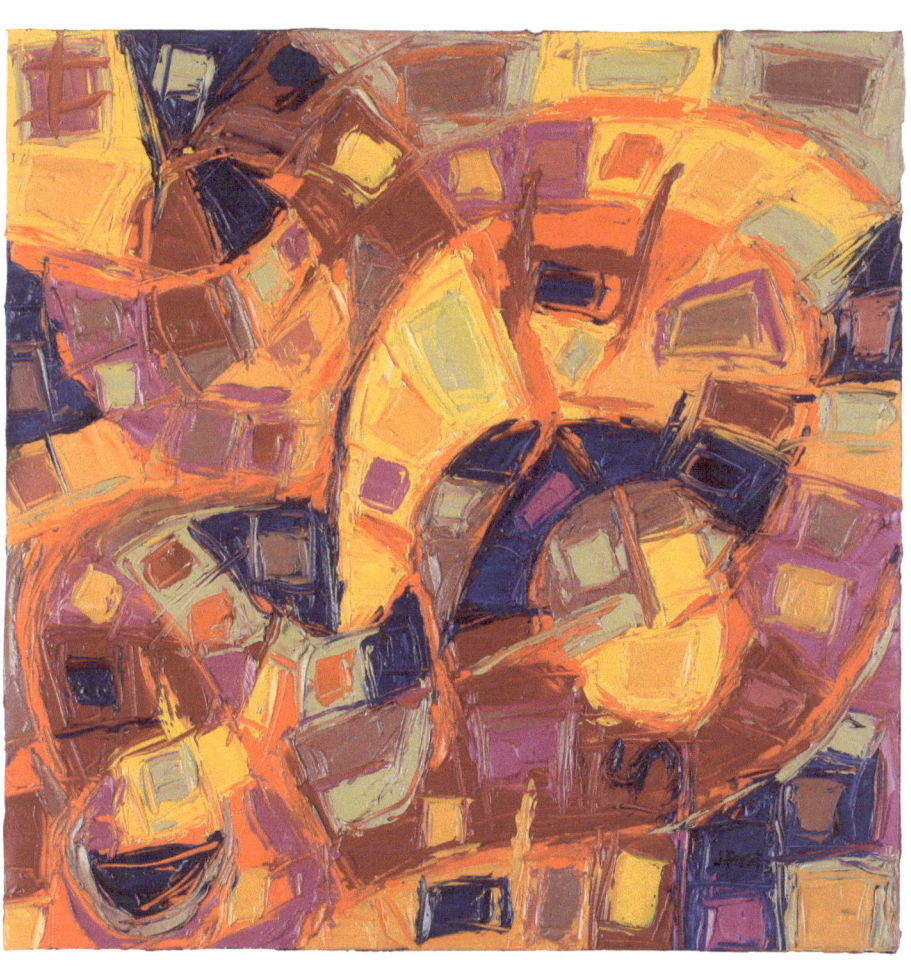

Concerto in D Minor
24 x 24 inches
Oil on canvas
2009

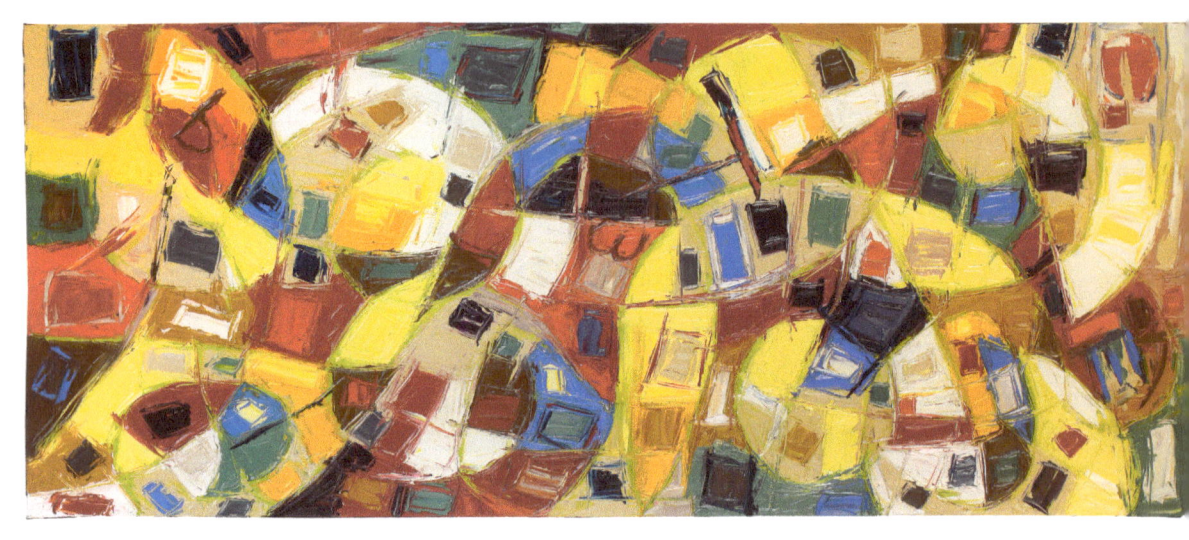

Garden of Eden
36 x 84 inches
Oil on canvas
2010

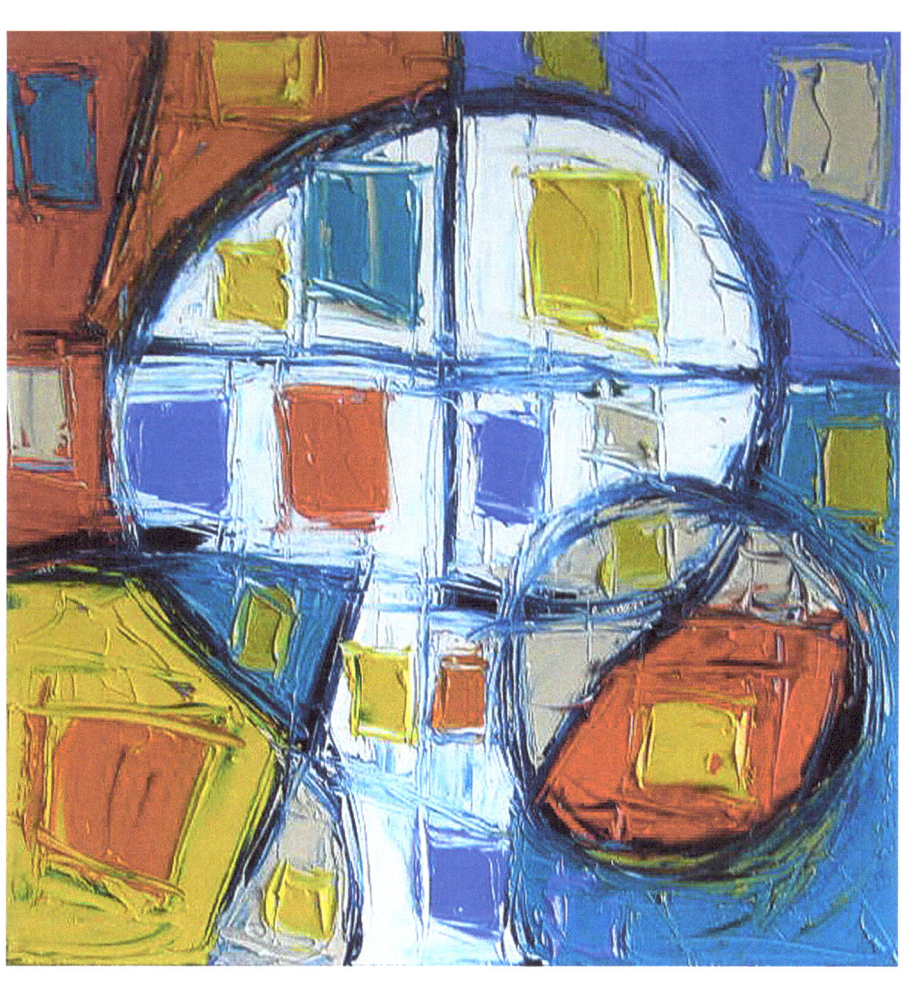

OMG
16 x 16 inches
Oil on canvas
2009

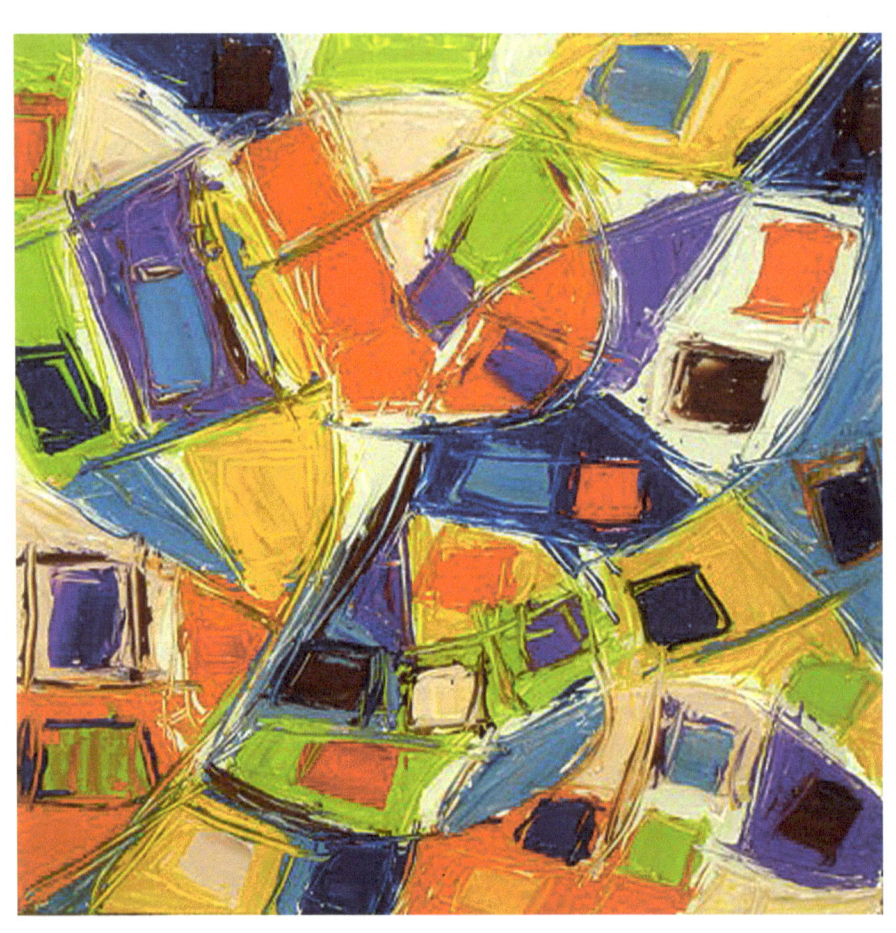

Caribbean #1
16 x 16 inches
Oil on canvas
2009

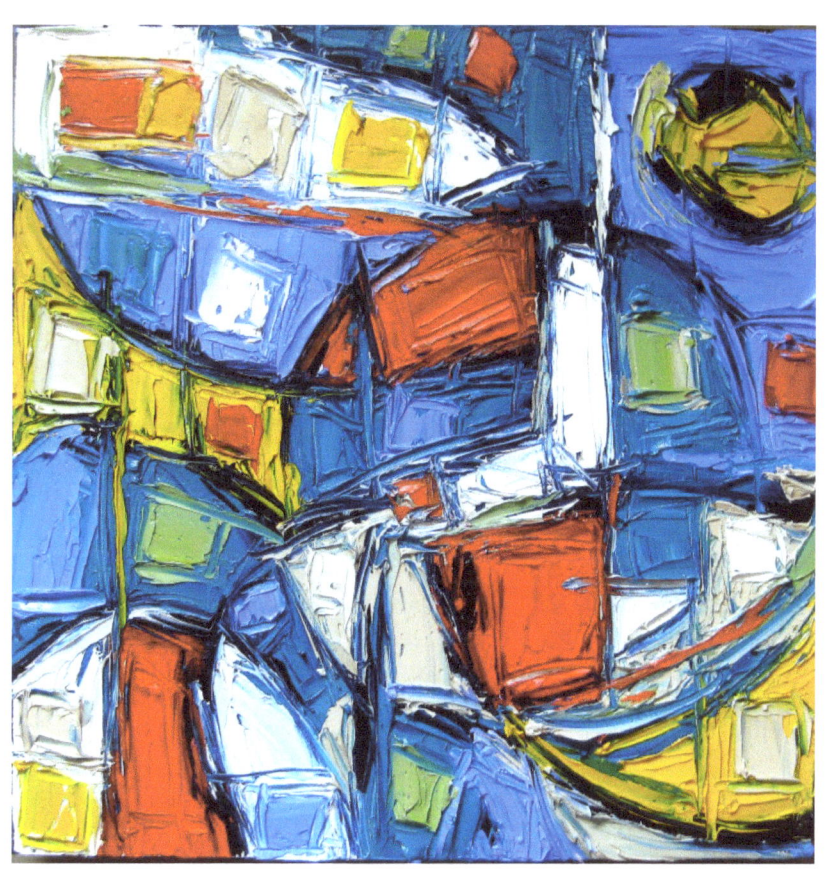

Summer Sailing
16 x 16 inches
Oil on canvas
2009

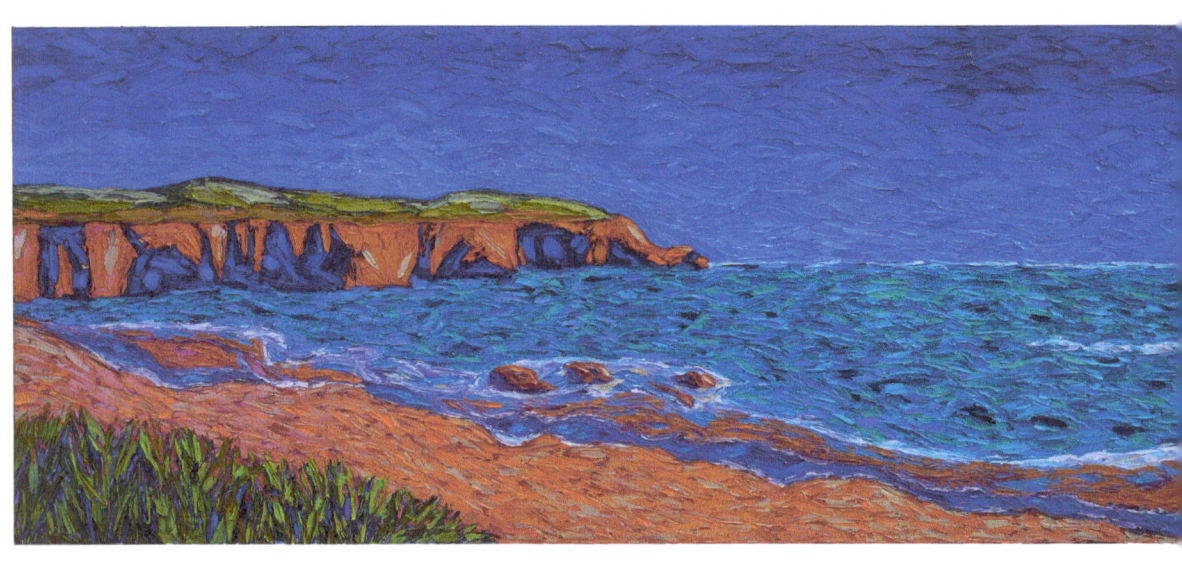

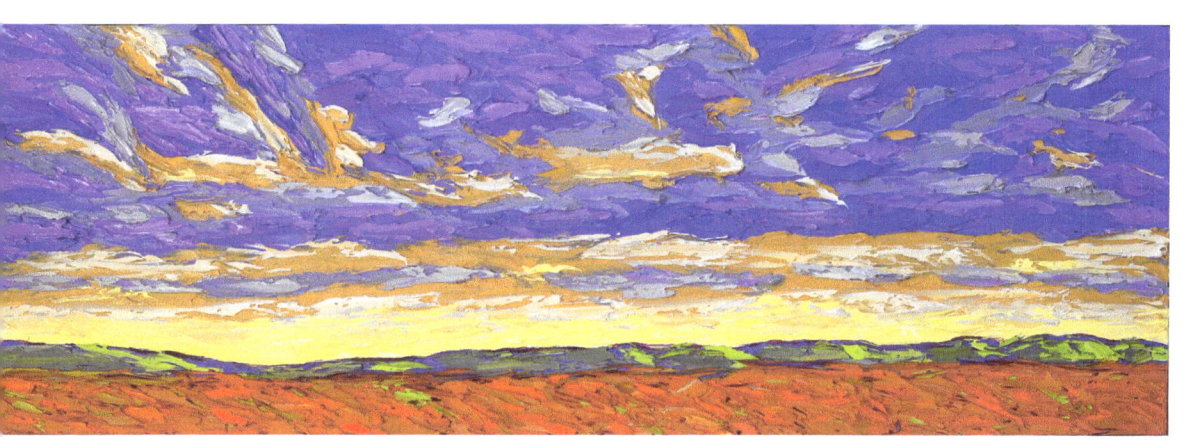

After the Storm
16 x 48 inches
Oil on canvas
2010

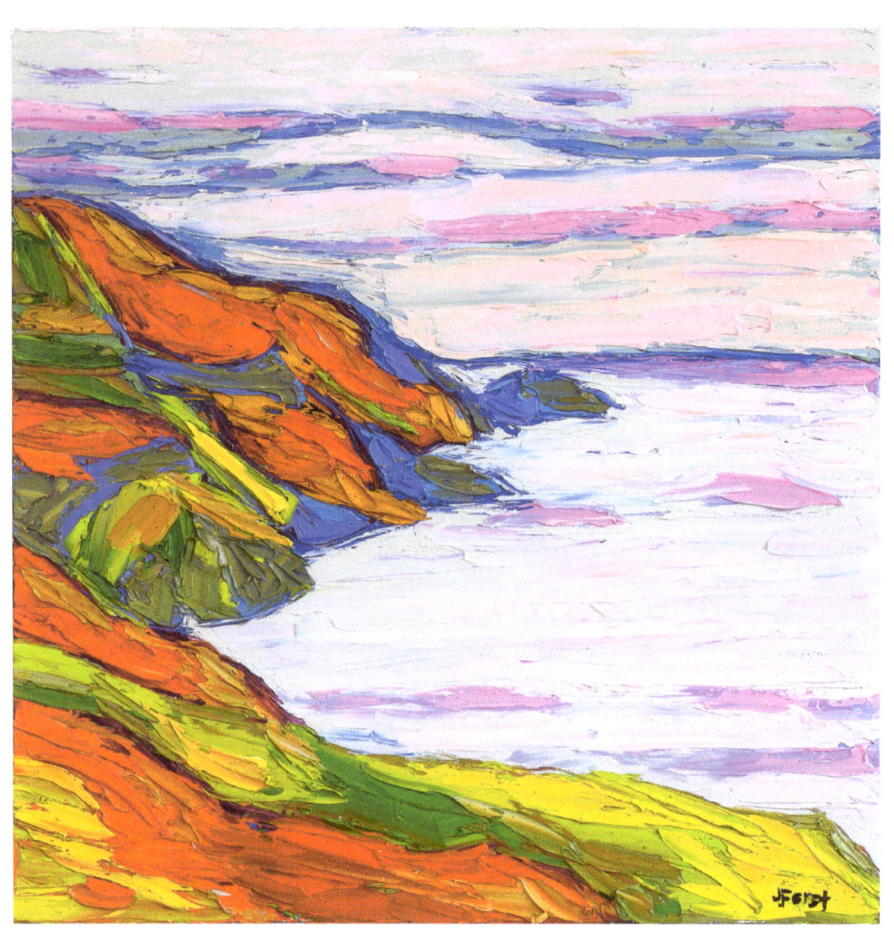

Coastal Landscape
24 x 24 inches
Oil on canvas
2010

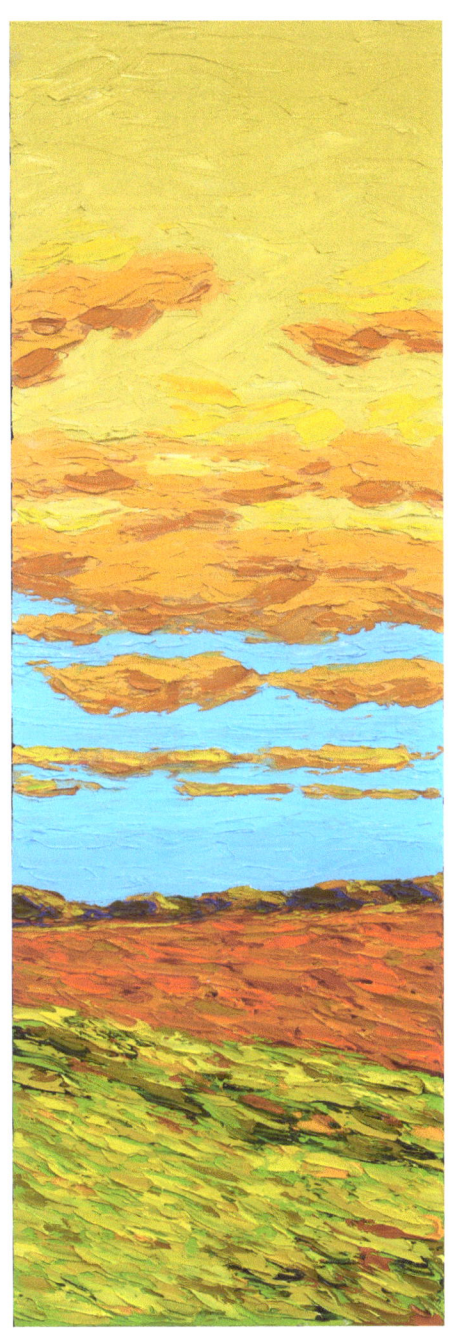

Early Morning
48 x 16 inches
Oil on canvas
2010

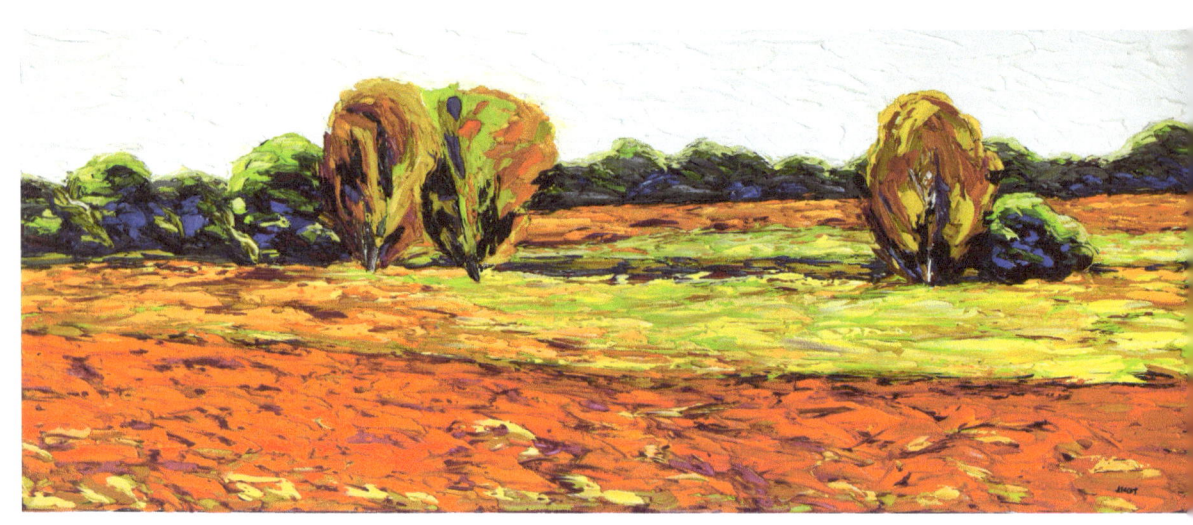

Summer Breeze
24 x 60 inches
Oil on canvas
2010

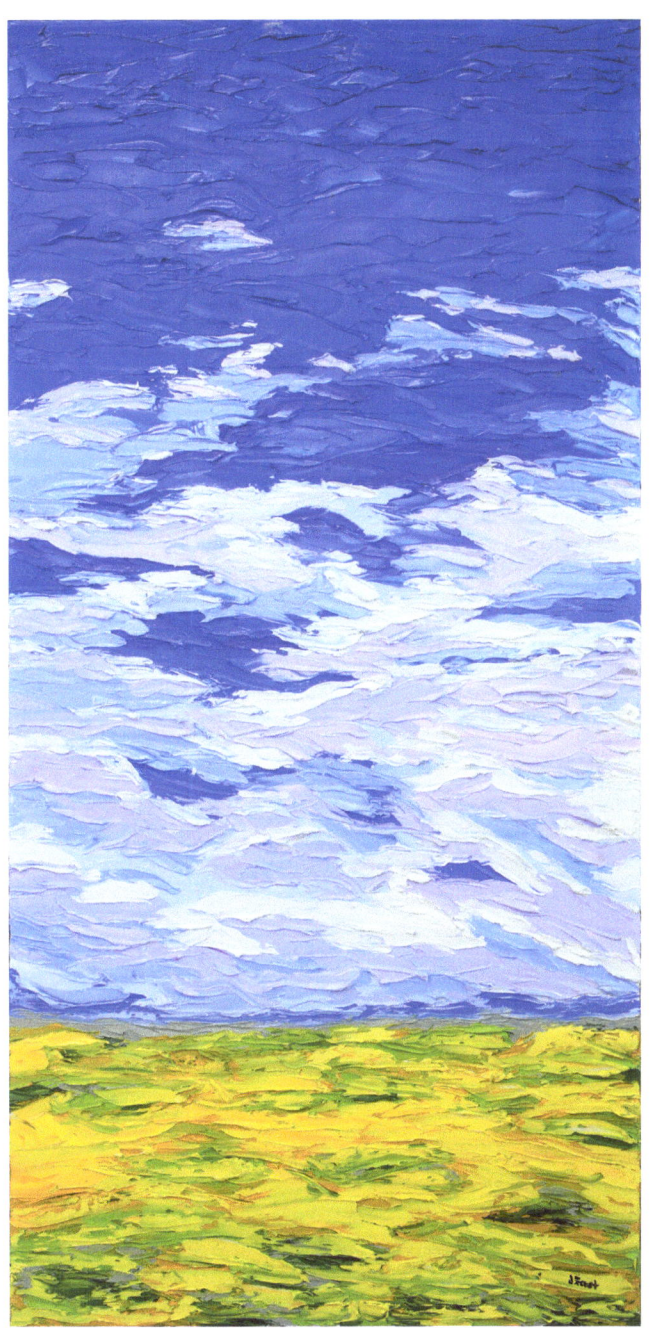

Lazy Days
60 x 30 inches
Oil on canvas
2010

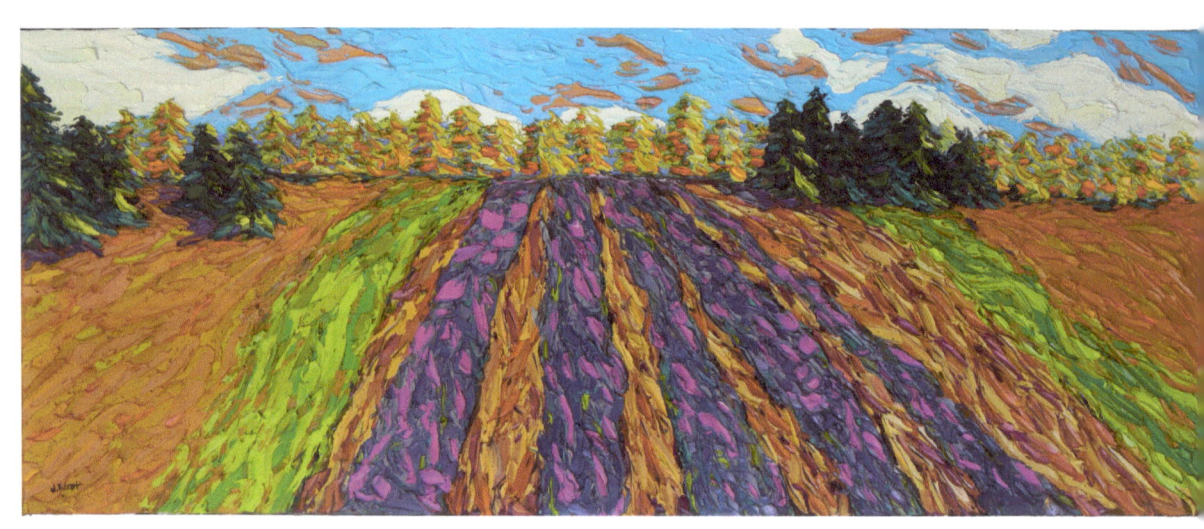

Field of Flowers
24 x 60 inches
Oil on canvas
2010

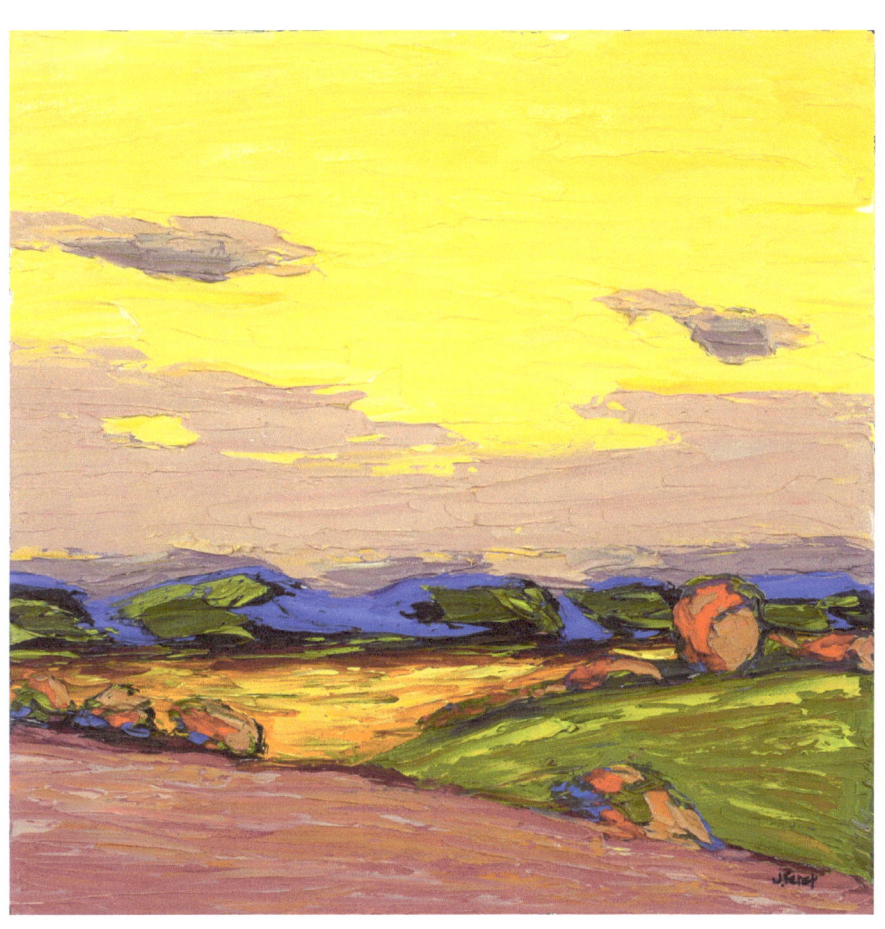

A Pastoral View
24 x 24 inches
Oil on canvas
2010

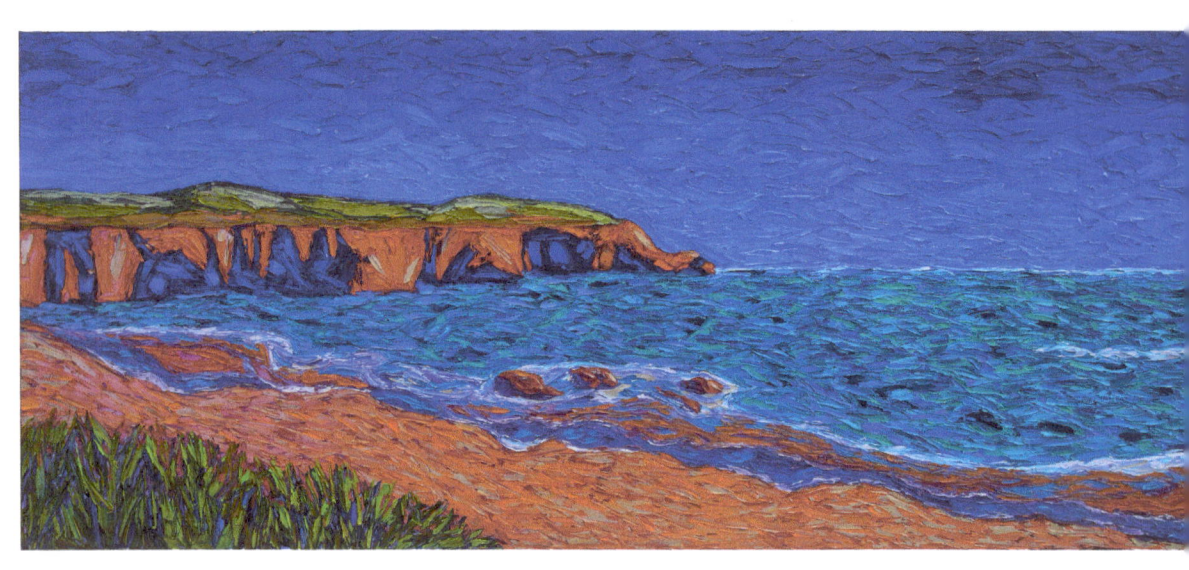

Silent Shore
36x 84 inches
Oil on canvas
2010

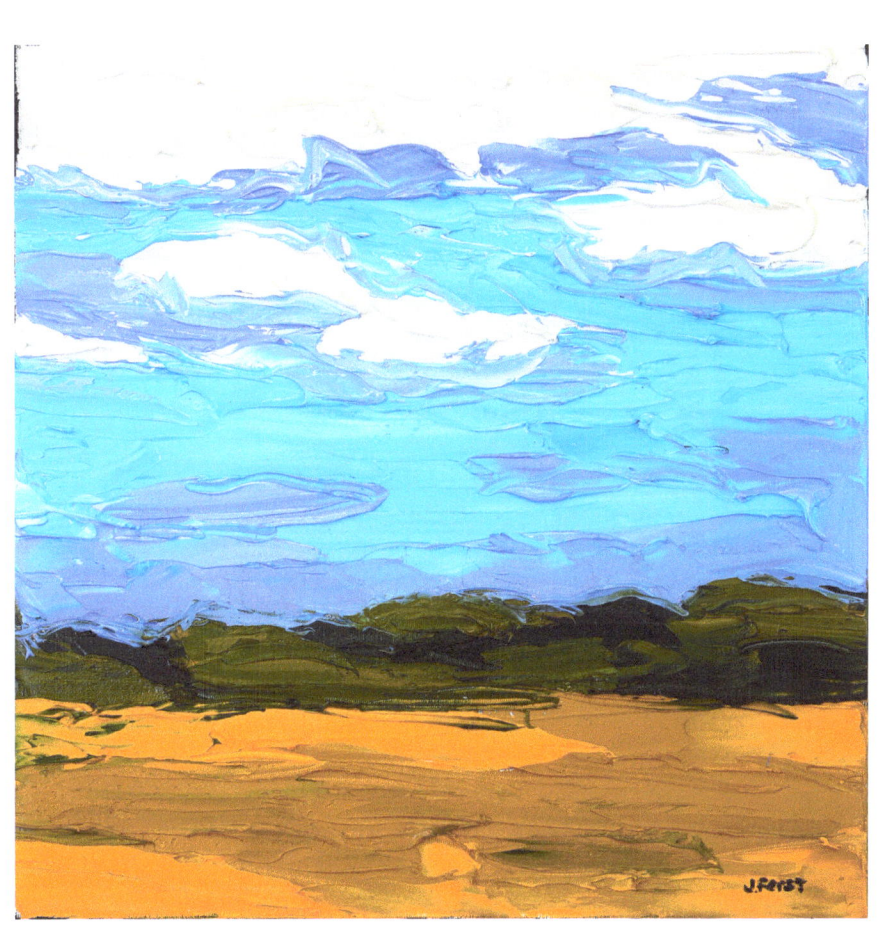

Wheat Field
16 x 16 inches
Oil on canvas
2010

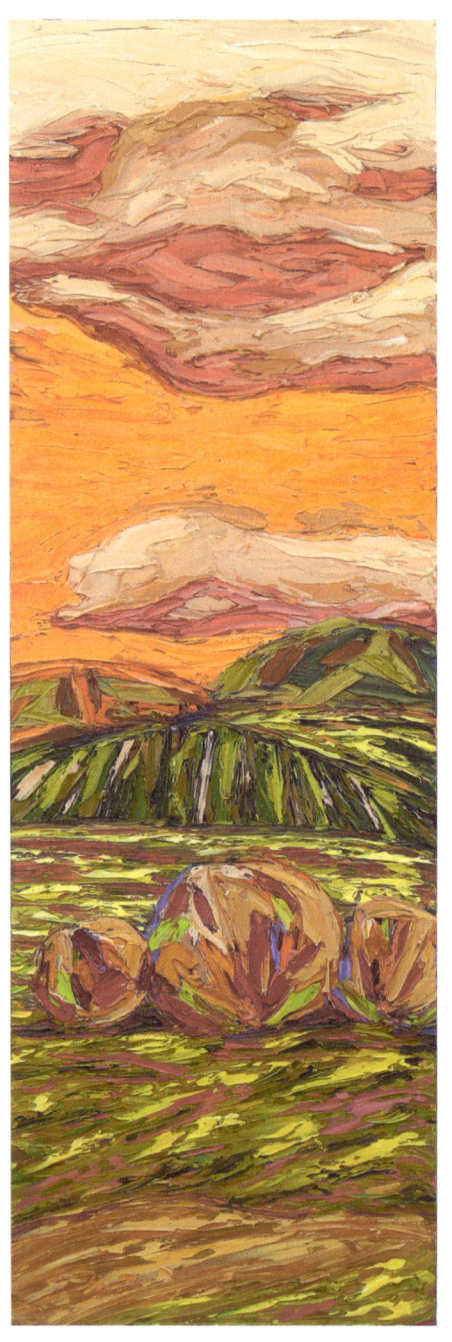

Wildflowers
48 x 16 inches
Oil on canvas
2010

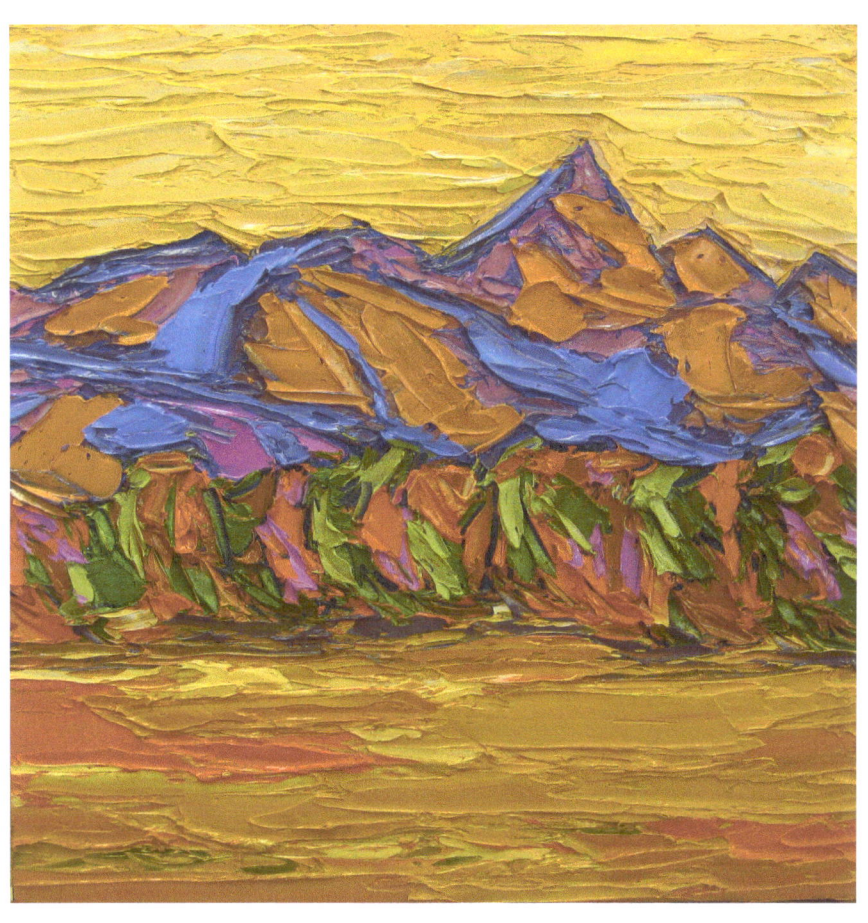

Grand Teton at Sunset
16 x 16 inches
Oil on canvas
2010

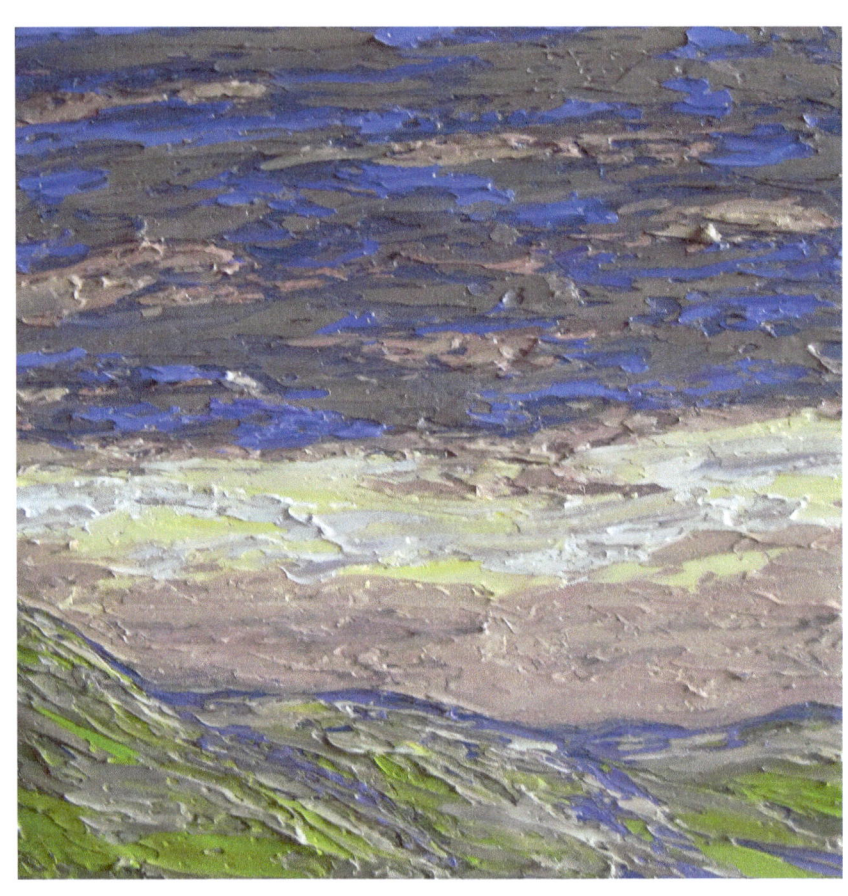

Sailing By the Italian Coast
16 x 16 inches
Oil on canvas
2010